# SpringerBriefs in Computer Science

For further volumes:
http://www.springer.com/series/10028

Michał Wódczak

# Autonomic Computing Enabled Cooperative Networked Design

 Springer

Michał Wódczak
Poznań, Poland

ISSN 2191-5768          ISSN 2191-5776 (electronic)
ISBN 978-1-4939-0763-2   ISBN 978-1-4939-0764-9 (eBook)
DOI 10.1007/978-1-4939-0764-9
Springer New York Heidelberg Dordrecht London

Library of Congress Control Number: 2014934566

Printed on acid-free paper

Springer is part of Springer Science+Business Media (www.springer.com)

# Preface

The emergence of the visionary concept of autonomic computing may be perceived as a sign of the times. Having been inspired by the workings of the human autonomic nervous system, this groundbreaking technology was soon after elevated even further to embrace the very world of networking. In particular, as described in the first chapter, while this book introduces the concept of autonomic computing driven cooperative networked system, it leverages and capitalises on the relevant advancements in both the realms of computing and networking by welding them closely together and, thus, making the proposed solution as multi-faceted as it is convergent. In fact, a novel Autonomic Cooperative System Architectural Model is defined which introduces the notion of Autonomic Cooperative Behaviour being orchestrated by the Autonomic Cooperative Networking Protocol of a cross-layer nature. Given such a context, not only does the book account for the needs of incorporating certain Decision Making Entities to facilitate the overall system operation, but it also provides the necessary implementation guidelines along with the pertinent standardisation orientated insight.

More specifically, the second chapter presents the very concept of autonomic computing, as well as its further translation into the domain of modern networking. Being of a context setting nature, the chapter provides an extensive commentary and analysis to outline the current status and role of autonomics overall. The main emphasis is put on the explanation of the transposition of the human Autonomic Nervous System (ANS) into the architecture for managing complex computer systems. Not only are the key aspects of the original approach explained but also the conceptual changes are indicated to settle the ground for the introduction of the new concept of Autonomic Cooperative System Architectural Model (ACSAM).

Next, the third chapter outlines the workings of ACSAM with special emphasis put on its novelty with regard to the Generic Autonomic Network Architecture (GANA). A special attention is paid to the bottom-up analysis of Autonomic Control Loops (ACLs) operating on various levels of abstraction. As a result, the key components of the said ACSAM, in the form of the Autonomic Cooperative Networking Protocol (ACNP) and Autonomic Cooperative Behaviour (ACB), are introduced, to be further analysed in the chapters to follow. In particular, at this stage the reader is familiarised with the key concept of Autonomic Cooperative Node (ACN) being the main enabler for the instantiation of the said ACB.

The fourth chapter details the very concept of ACB constituting the lowest level of the three-tier ACSAM and designed as being composed with the aid of creating Virtual Cooperative Sets (VCSs), orchestrated by the Autonomic Cooperative Networking Protocol. In fact, not only is ACB many-faceted but it is also hardly definable. To account for its role and meaning, the notion of collaborative and supportive protocols is introduced and the Virtual Multiple Input Multiple Output (VMIMO) channel is defined as its enabler through the Distributed Spatio-Temporal Block Coding (DSTBC) over VCSs and with the aid of the Multi-Point Relay (MPR) station selection heuristics of the Optimised Link State Routing (OLSR) protocol.

In the fifth chapter the workings of the Autonomic Cooperative Networking Protocol are outlined. As such, the ACNP is a cross-layer protocol combining certain aspects of both the Network Layer and Link Layer, in fact, going down even to the Physical Layer for the orchestration of the underlying VMIMO. In particular, the relevant context of the reference OLSR protocol is presented and the integration of ACB is described keeping in mind the role of the MPR station selection heuristics. This part is complemented with the proposed messaging structure and the functioning of ACNP itself in terms of assigning ACNs to VCSs. Eventually, the analysis of the expected overhead induced by the OLSR-ACNP tandem is provided.

The sixth chapter introduces the Decision Making Entities to complement the overall ACSAM. First, the Cooperative Transmission Decision Element CT_DE is deployed at the protocol level to orchestrate the VMIMO enabled DSTBC. Then, certain logic is elevated to the function level, where the Cooperation Management Decision Element CM_DE is located, interacting with ACNP to enable the MPR-based VCSs. Moving up to the node level, the Cooperative Re-Routing Decision Element CR_DE is introduced triggering cooperative re-routing to guarantee service continuity. Last but not least is the network level Cooperation Orchestration Decision Element CO_DE responsible for arranging various ACB accordingly.

Next, the seventh chapter provides the insight into the practical side of the ACSAM and is related to the implementation and simulation aspects. To this end, the architecture of the developed simulator is introduced along with the operational aspects of the protocol itself. Based on this, the concept of multi-threading with the use of the Java programming language is discussed to show its direct correspondence with the notion of Autonomic Cooperative Behaviour. This part is further complemented with the mathematical analysis of the reception of the DSTBC, and, finally, the parameters of the assumed scenario are described together with the corresponding layouts of ACNs and the reference simulation results.

Finally, the eighth chapter analyses both the standardisation and deployment orientated concepts. First, the Autonomic Future Internet is discussed with the emphasis put on standardisation within the Industry Specification Group (ISG) on Autonomic network engineering for the self-managing Future Internet (AFI), functioning under the auspices of the European Telecommunications Standards Institute (ETSI). Then, the Machine-to-Machine (M2M) communications are analysed also in the context of ETSI and the concept of Software Defined Networking (SDN) follows. Eventually, both the Emergency Systems and Vehicular Networks are brought up to present certain architectural advancements from the deployment viewpoint.

Poznań, Poland                                                          Michał Wódczak

# Contents

# Acronyms

| | |
|---|---|
| **AB** | Autonomic Behaviour |
| **AC** | Autonomic Computing |
| **ACB** | Autonomic Cooperative Behaviour |
| **ACL** | Autonomic Control Loop |
| **ACSAM** | Autonomic Cooperative System Architectural Model |
| **ACN** | Autonomic Cooperative Node |
| **ACNP** | Autonomic Cooperative Networking Protocol |
| **ADME** | Autonomic Decision Making Element |
| **AE** | Autonomic Element |
| **AF** | Amplify-and-Forward |
| **AFI** | Autonomic network engineering for the self-managing Future Internet |
| **AI** | Artificial Intelligence |
| **AM** | Autonomic Manager |
| **AN** | Autonomic Networking |
| **AN** | Autonomic Node |
| **ANCS** | Autonomic Networked Computing System |
| **ANS** | Autonomic Nervous System |
| **ARP** | Address Resolution Protocol |
| **AS** | Autonomic System |
| **AWGN** | Additive White Gaussian Noise |
| **BER** | Bit Error Rate |
| **BS** | Base Station |
| **CBR** | Constant Bit Rate |
| **CDF** | Cumulative Distribution Function |
| **CLI** | Command Line Interface |
| **CFR** | Chief First Responder |
| **CPU** | Central Processing Unit |
| **CRR** | Cooperative Re-Routing |
| **DE** | Decision Element |
| **DF** | Decode-and-Forward |
| **DME** | Decision Making Element |

| | |
|---|---|
| **DME** | Decision Making Entity |
| **DN** | Destination Node |
| **DR** | Decode-and-Reencode |
| **DSTBC** | Distributed Spatio-Temporal Block Coding |
| **ECMP** | Equal Cost Multipath Protocol |
| **EOC** | Emergency Operations Centre |
| **ETSI** | European Telecommunications Standards Institute |
| **FR** | First Responder |
| **FRR** | Fast Re-Routing |
| **GANA** | Generic Autonomic Network Architecture |
| **GS** | Group Specification |
| **GUI** | Graphical User Interface |
| **HCL** | Hierarchical Control Loop |
| **HRP** | Horizontal Reference Point |
| **HTT** | Hyper-Threading Technology |
| **IoT** | Internet of Things |
| **IP** | Internet Protocol |
| **ISG** | Industry Specification Group |
| **LAN** | Local Area Network |
| **LOS** | Line of Sight |
| **LSB** | Least Significant Bit |
| **M2M** | Machine-to-Machine |
| **MAC** | Medium Access Control |
| **MAS** | Multi-Agent System |
| **MANET** | Mobile Ad-hoc NETwork |
| **ME** | Managed Element |
| **ME** | Managed Entity |
| **MEA** | Multi-Element Array |
| **MEOC** | Mobile Emergency Operations Centre |
| **MIMO** | Multiple Input Multiple Output |
| **MPR** | Multi-Point Relay |
| **MSB** | Most Significant Bit |
| **NLOS** | Non Line-of-Sight |
| **OBU** | On-Board Unit |
| **OFDMA** | Orthogonal Frequency Division Multiple Access |
| **OLSR** | Optimised Link State Routing |
| **OSI** | Open Systems Interconnection |
| **PAN** | Personal Area Network |
| **QoS** | Quality of Service |
| **QPSK** | Quadrature Phase Shift Keying |
| **RA** | Reference Architecture |
| **RAN** | Radio Access Network |
| **RAP** | Radio Access Point |
| **REACT** | Routing information Enhanced Algorithm for Cooperative Transmission |

| | |
|---|---|
| **RM** | Reference Model |
| **RN** | Relay Node |
| **SDN** | Software Defined Networking |
| **SN** | Source Node |
| **SINR** | Signal-to-Interference-plus-Noise Ratio |
| **SNR** | Signal-to-Noise Ratio |
| **SOA** | Service Oriented Architecture |
| **STBC** | Spatio-Temporal Block Coding |
| **SVD** | Singular Value Decomposition |
| **TCO** | Total Cost of Ownership |
| **TCP/IP** | Transmission Control Protocol/Internet Protocol |
| **TDD** | Time Division Duplex |
| **TTL** | Time To Live |
| **TS** | Technical Specification |
| **UDP** | User Datagram Protocol |
| **VAA** | Virtual Antenna Array |
| **VANET** | Vehicular Ad-hoc NETwork |
| **VCS** | Virtual Cooperative Set |
| **VMIMO** | Virtual Multiple Input Multiple Output |
| **VMISO** | Virtual Multiple Input Single Output |
| **VRP** | Vertical Reference Point |
| **WI** | Work Item |

# Chapter 1
# Introduction

As the number of devices interconnected worldwide is growing drastically, the question of the orchestration of a durability-orientated operation of the related networked system becomes critically substantial. In fact, such a durability, understood in the context of the overall system resilience, may be most directly translated into the provision of the key features of reliability, availability, safety, confidentiality, integrity, and maintainability. For this reason, the book advocates for the integration of cooperative networking with the rationale behind autonomic computing in terms of self-management expressed through self-configuration, self-optimisation, self-healing, and self-protection. In particular, the concept of Autonomic Cooperative System Architectural Model (ACSAM) is proposed which is based on the introduction of the Autonomic Cooperative Networking Protocol (ACNP) together with its pertinent Autonomic Cooperative Behaviour (ACB). As such, looking from the lowest level perspective, the component of Autonomic Cooperative Behaviour may be perceived as stemming from and being triggered by the concept of Distributed Spatio-Temporal Block Coding (DSTBC), primarily aiming to enable collaboration among networked devices, yet being enhanced with the integration of the relevant network layer routines in form of the modified Multi-Point Relay (MPR) station selection heuristics. Obviously, while the system grows, it appears natural, at least from the local scope perspective, to instantiate such a cross-layer integration of the aspects of collaboration with the use of a network layer protocol in order to limit any unnecessary control overhead resulting from the exchange of data among the networked devices, as performed with the aid of the said Autonomic Cooperative Networking Protocol. However, going further, since today's distributed systems are becoming more and more complex, the transition from the local to a more global perspective requires, in addition, the incorporation of an autonomic overlay so that the routing information enabled distributed cooperative system could self-manage on a global scale. This way, networked devices may improve system durability by sharing their capabilities and resources for the needs of expressing and instantiating the Autonomic Cooperative Behaviour. In fact, the paradigm of autonomic system design assumes that such a networked set-up

M. Wódczak, *Autonomic Computing Enabled Cooperative Networked Design*,
SpringerBriefs in Computer Science, DOI 10.1007/978-1-4939-0764-9_1,
© The Author(s) 2014

should follow the operating principles of the human autonomic nervous system and, thus, be able to exercise full self-management without any external intervention. Consequently, thanks to the proposed Autonomic Cooperative System Architectural Model, both the cooperation and autonomics are immediately becoming welded closely together into a joint concept to offer best Quality of Service (QoS) under the assumption of strictly following any externally or internally imposed policies. The resulting networked set-up is then assumed to feature the capability of analysing the current context and making an attempt to benefit from the advantage of having incorporated the above-mentioned concepts for the benefit of the overall durable and resilient system operation.

# Chapter 2
# Autonomic Computing and Networking

## 2.1 Introduction

This chapter presents the rationale behind the introduction of the visionary concept of autonomic computing, as well as its rapidly progressing further translation into and convergence with the domain of modern networked systems. Even though it could be perceived as being more of an introductory, context setting nature only, in fact the chapter provides an extensive, additional commentary and analysis for the purpose of outlining the most comprehensive view on the current status and role of autonomics overall. To this end, not only are the key aspects of the original approach explained but the relevant conceptual and architectural changes are indicated to settle the ground for the introduction of the new concept of Autonomic Cooperative System Architectural Model (ACSAM). In particular, after the general vision has been introduced, the main emphasis is put on the explanation of the workings of the original approach advocating for the transposition of the human Autonomic Nervous System (ANS) into the architecture responsible for the management of complex computer systems. This involves the introduction of the aspects of self-configuration, self-optimisation, self-healing, and self-protection, altogether constituting the notion of self-management. The pertinent architectural assumptions and variations follow and are expanded into the discussion regarding the complementary nature of autonomics and agent systems. Finally, the very issue of convergence is brought up together with the role of self-awareness with regard to the target autonomic networked computer system.

## 2.2 Vision and Conceptual Correspondence

The emergence of the visionary concept of autonomic computing may be perceived as a sign of the times. Even though the idea of automation has been strived after for a couple of decades, the real outbreak of a tangible advancement in

M. Wódczak, *Autonomic Computing Enabled Cooperative Networked Design*,
SpringerBriefs in Computer Science, DOI 10.1007/978-1-4939-0764-9_2,
© The Author(s) 2014

this field appears to coincide with the beginning of the twenty-first century [10]. Such a situation may be attributed to a stunningly rapid development of highly complex distributed systems, comprising a multitude of interconnected devices, each running complicated software and, thus, posing serious demands in terms of proper configuration and timely maintenance. In fact, initially, the concept of autonomics targeted primarily computer systems, however, as it will be shown throughout the remainder of this book, many crucial architectural variations have been devised thus welding both the realms of computing and networking very closely together [9].

Interestingly, the idea of autonomic computing was inspired the by the way the natural human Autonomic Nervous System operates the body related parameters, such as heart rate or temperature, thereby releasing the brain from controlling them in a fully aware manner [6]. In fact, there is a plethora of such parameters which are considered crucial for the overall functioning of the human organism, yet, a bit surprisingly, the process of control is performed in a somewhat detached and distributed fashion [10]. The organisation of such an autonomic system is said to resemble a recursively arranged hierarchy where each of the numerous self-governing components on a given level encompasses numerous, conceptually similar yet functionally varying, components on a lower level and so forth [6]. In other words, it naturally follows similar patterns understood in a more abstract way, starting from the molecular level, going through human markets and societies, and ending up at the global world's socio-economy [6].

While making an attempt at identifying the reasons for the emergence of autonomics, one may come to a conclusion that, in fact, it is the complexity to serve as its key enabler. In particular, as such complex systems are very demanding in terms of maintenance, there appears to be an urgent need for the application of self-monitoring and self-healing in order to enable the possibility of bypassing their potential malfunctions without any specific human intervention, at least over the majority of time [10]. From the practical point of view, as already mentioned, this issue pertains to the question of the composition of an autonomic computer networked system both in terms of software and hardware. In particular, a system is referred to which encompasses both the self-managing operating systems and intelligent software, as well as redundant memory and processors equipped with self-healing firmware [10]. In this case, however, autonomics is realised through redundancy while, in general, it is especially expected to manifest itself through proper system configuration in the first place.

In fact, nowadays software has become not only a ubiquitous and common commodity but, most of all, a particularly highly complex one. It is so especially for critical applications where any risk of failure may be catastrophic when the consequences are concerned. To mitigate any such effects, certain organisations are claimed to spend even 33–50 % of the Total Cost of Ownership (TCO) of their related computing and communication infrastructure in order to avoid any such software malfunction [5]. It is then believed that only a holistic and systemic approach could be of a value in such a case and, consequently, the concept of self-managing software is advocated for, calling for self-direction, self-governance, and self-adaptation [5]. This idea is, most obviously, tightly bound with self-managing hardware, where the very same principles of complexity apply, both at the microscopic and macroscopic levels. In particular, this pertains to interconnected computers forming vast and distributed systems, where the notion of self-management interweaves software and hardware.

All in all, usually there are three reasons referred to when the enablers for the advent of autonomic computing are sought for [1]. First of all, the complexity of networked computer systems is mentioned including topics such as highly demanding and complicated database management systems, where the multitude of parameters to be configured has become substantial, if not overwhelming, thus posing certain orchestration issues. Secondly, the commercial development and the resulting considerably vast deployment of Service Oriented Architecture (SOA) adds another dimension of complexity to the above issue, as the distribution of system components often means they are no longer under the command of a single organisation understood in a wide sense. Last but not least comes the very feature of heterogeneity of both software and hardware, not to mention the services offered with their aid. This way the today's networked computing systems are becoming more of a melting pot of an enormous variety of concepts and solutions, thereby calling for the incorporation of the notion of autonomics to facilitate self-management.

The aforementioned issue of autonomic system complexity may become one of its most critical characteristics in terms of proper self-maintenance understood as the, de facto, self-management to be further elaborated on in the following section. Most obviously, such complexity calls for a special treatment and, in fact, it was proposed to be tackled with and orchestrated by the application of an economics and artificial intelligence related mathematical device of utility functions devised to serve as a means of facilitating the specification of preferences [7]. In particular, the utility functions allow to specify a multitude of parameters based on which a learned decision or decisions may be taken by an ADME.[1] By all means does the notion of a learned decision making require the acquisition and processing of the relevant information for the needs of accumulating knowledge [15]. At the same time, the said parameters are claimed to most directly translate into resource-level indicators or, going further, straightforwardly into their related QoS metrics, intended not only to allow for and facilitate the formulation of the optimisation function but, most of all, the identification of the ways and methods of, first, addressing the complexity issue, and, then, solving it, as advocated for in [7].

---

[1]More precisely, originally "rational decisions" of "automated agents" are referred to in this context [7]. The description provided in the book, however, is already targeted towards and adjusted with the theory behind the Generic Autonomic Network Architecture (GANA) to be presented in the next chapter [2].

## 2.3   Notion and Constituents of Self-Management

In principle, autonomics assumes the exclusion of any human involvement, in fact meaning the one of an administrator, from a rather demanding and time-consuming task of a computer system operation and maintenance. Being able to function without having to be overseen, such a system is then expected to self-manage, thus providing the end users with uninterrupted peak performance [6]. In other words, the system should observe the internal and external conditions, as well as software and hardware issues, and take actions to address them properly. This may include, for example, the process of obtaining software updates, installing them, reconfiguring if necessary, running tests, and, potentially, reverting the previous software version as it may turn out inevitable and necessary in the case of errors [6]. Most precisely, such functionality may be achieved through the use of the following four key characteristic components of the concept of self-management, i.e.: self-configuration, self-optimisation, self-healing, and self-protection, as depicted in Fig. 2.1.

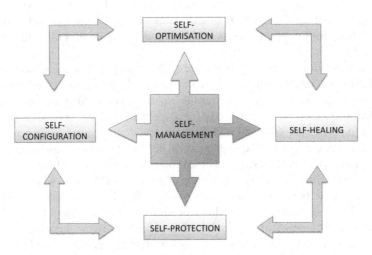

**Fig. 2.1**  Self-management

In particular, first of all the self-configuration related component is empha-sised which pertains directly to the multitude of software and hardware solutions developed and delivered by different vendors, including system elements such as databases, routers, or servers [6]. Given the aforementioned complexity of the cur-rently devised computer systems, the relevant configuration of new equipment may by critically time-consuming, especially when certain unexpected and not easily solvable interoperability issues arise. This aspect becomes especially crucial in the case of widespread set-ups, where the overwhelming number of devices renders manual configuration not only virtually impossible but also highly impractical.

In the first place, an autonomic system is then expected to identify its own capabilities, as well as the properties of a given new component and use some relevant high-level policies for the needs of a proper configuration.

Most obviously, self-configuration goes hand in hand with self-optimisation which should be perceived in terms of parameter tuning, both in the case of software and hardware. Especially, for this very component, the software inherent parameters should not be accidentally confused with the hardware related ones, even though, in both cases, the tuning may be perceived as a purely software driven process. In particular, as the number of parameters is claimed to increase with every system release, the task of self-optimisation similarly appears almost unattainable without the application of some relevantly adjusted autonomic routines [6]. What is more, self-optimisation is not only intended to take place when a new software or hardware component has been attached to the system. Quite the contrary, this process should be continuous as it is the case for the aforementioned Autonomic Nervous System so that modifications could be made on the fly, mostly as a result of being facilitated by certain additionally instrumented learning and reasoning processes and capabilities.

Once the system has carried out and successfully accomplished the above-mentioned tasks of self-configuration and self-optimisation,[2] it requires to be properly monitored in order to accommodate yet another key feature, i.e. the one related to self-healing. The rationale behind the capability of monitoring stems from the fact that the highly and rapidly increasing complexity of the currently deployed networked computer systems poses certain difficulty in identifying, tracing, and determining the very root cause or causes of a given problem or group of, potentially related, incidents [6]. Non-autonomic approaches may take up to several weeks of a difficult and demanding analysis and result in a highly tangible diagnosis, not to mention the case when the cause or problem has suddenly disappeared [6]. Apparently, such an approach belongs to the resilience related class of solutions where the system might observe certain incidents still before a problem has occurred in order to undertake any relevant action well in advance, thus potentially avoiding otherwise imminent complications [16].

Moreover, the requirement of self-healing is very deeply correlated with self-protection, at the same time exposing certain dose of similarity to fault-management. In fact, due to the mutual relations between resilience and fault-management, the idea of inferring on the basis of symptoms, as indicated previously for the case of self-healing, is undoubtedly maybe even more pertinent to the task of self-protection. In other words, the system is expected to autonomically detect and resolve any unexpected malicious attacks or cascading failures [6]. This way, the data collected during the phase of monitoring may be properly filtered in order to pinpoint the potential root causes and, thus, reason on the yet unknown but sufficiently probable problems, potentially to come. While self-protection should provide the measures necessary for a widely understood failure avoidance, mostly

---

[2]In fact, such tasks rather appear to be continuous processes, as the configuration may be changing dynamically and adaptively over time, triggering not only self-optimisation but also self-protection.

consisting in problem mitigation, the routine of self-healing appears to be more of a remedial nature [16]. It means, in turn, that both mechanisms need to interact and base their operation on the aforementioned tasks of self-configuration and self-optimisation.

Obviously, such functionality may only be attained gradually and it is assumed that, initially, all the above-mentioned components would need to be considered and deployed separately. Even though, with the passage of time, self-configuration, self-optimisation, self-healing, and self-protection could become more and more welded together, this process would need to additionally accommodate the evolution of the said self-management understood in a more generic way, as a consistent concept [6]. In other words, first, autonomics would solely help in collecting the data that an administrator could use as a support for the decision making process. Following, the role of autonomic control processes would be expected to be elevated to the level of suggesting certain actions to the human, and, finally, such processes would function in an entirely standalone and detached fashion, basing their own decisions on the actions of some other relevant lower level control processes [6].

**Fig. 2.2** Autonomic computing levels

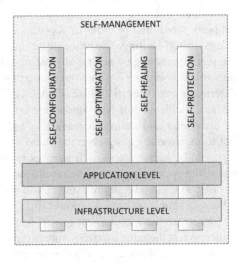

Going further, the presumably horizontal arrangement of the constituents of self-management in the form of self-configuration, self-optimisation, self-healing, and self-protection would need to be perceived from two angles, or, rather, from two levels. In fact, as depicted in Fig. 2.2, the autonomic functions need to be performed at both the application and infrastructure levels [1]. This vertical separation and arrangement appears to be very much in line with the aforementioned close relation, if not in a tangible overlapping, between the realms of computing and networking, where certain aspects advocating for the deployment of automation are, in fact, stemming from the very same root concepts behind the autonomic system design. The main driver for such a separation is the proper maintenance of a sufficient separation between software and hardware, which, on the other hand, may pose certain additional difficulty, as, nowadays, more and more hardware appears to carry the "software-defined" label.

## 2.4  Architectural Assumptions and Variations

The very initial concept of Autonomic Computing (AC) assumes that a system expressing such a capability should comprise numerous so called Autonomic Elements (AEs), apparently being its most comprehensive, yet not entirely atomic constituents. In particular, AEs are expected to contain resources and deliver services while being able to manage their own behaviour and act pursuant to certain policies, either internal, i.e. imposed by other AEs, or external, i.e. imposed by humans [6]. Given the assumption of a continuous interaction, such an autonomic system is, in fact, claimed to be able to attain the level of a social intelligence of an example ant colony [6]. This does not necessarily impose any particular notion of being cognitive, as such an imitated colony is not a single organism. It is rather a collection of components notifying one another and acting according to directions or rules. As a result, the whole set-up may then work fairly smoothly by adapting itself to the current situation, even though, overall, it presumably lacks any awareness. In other words, the very principle of Autonomic Computing (AC) is reinforced once again by the above example as the ants could be compared to organs of a human body, interacting and exercising behaviour under the umbrella of the same "organism", of a more virtual nature in this very case, yet retaining its standalone components.

Interestingly, quite the contrary to the later developments aiming to capitalise on the concept of Autonomic Computing (AC), as further elaborated on in Chap. 3, the original solution was proposed under the assumption that the distributed decision making logic would be, in fact, encapsulated within the AEs.[3] As depicted in Fig. 2.3, an AE is composed of an Autonomic Manager (AM) and Managed Element (ME) remaining in a very close relation or, rather, interaction through the existence of the control loop which may work at a different pace [18].[4] It is crucial to note, however, that the inherent feature of each AE, at the same time being its central and focal point, is the notion of knowledge, surrounded by other relevant constituents. In particular, knowledge may be built upon certain pertinent data collected through monitoring and analysis. This is the ability which allows an AE to express some flavour of being able to reason through cognition. While reasoning may be more

---

[3]The current designs, such as the Generic Autonomic Network Architecture (GANA), appear to tend to rather expose the internals by modifying the notion of an Autonomic Element when perceived from the global perspective.

[4]Similarly, in the most recent developments the functionality equivalent to an ME is usually referred to as a Managed Entity (ME), while the legacy control loop functions rather as an Autonomic Control Loop (ACL).

**Fig. 2.3** Autonomic element

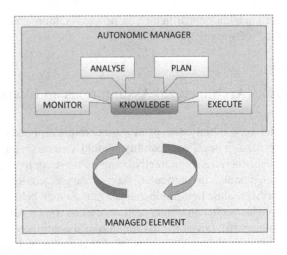

or less limited, it is assumed to manifest itself through tight and proper planning and execution. Planning, however, should incorporate, as its basis, not only the monitoring related data but, preferably, also the aforementioned relevant policies imposed either internally or externally.

Looking into the original design, as it was envisaged in [6], the currently evolved autonomic system architectures, such as the aforementioned GANA, naturally assume that the distinction between AM and ME is highly conceptual. In other words, especially on the higher levels of abstraction, comprising individual computing components, through entire automated enterprises, up to the global economy [6], the difference may be rather intangible, as the MEs could be equivalent to AEs.[5] Such an equivalence results from the fact that is it possible to take a direct control of any pertinent physical software or hardware components on the lowest level of the hierarchy only. In the majority of cases the entities located above are just intended to encapsulate certain logic which makes them very flexible in terms of the internal structure and the roles they are taking. They are then more containers facilitating the object-orientated system design from the architectural perspective, yet their functionality could be further split, shifted, or translated into some new functional blocks. The lowest level AEs, in turn, need to communicate with their MEs over, preferably standardised [17], interfaces thus making them more rigid, limited, and "hard-coded" in terms of the assumed design [6].

Regardless of the evolution stage of a particular instantiation of the concept of Autonomic Computing, however, it is clearly noticeable that both the original concept and the most recent development in the form of the Generic Autonomic

---

[5]For the sake of an immediate comparison, the GANA approach, orientated towards distributed networked systems, introduces four conceptual levels given here in the bottom–up order: protocol level, function level, node level, and network level, as introduced in Chap. 3 and further addressed in Chap. 6.

Network Architecture for distributed networked systems are very strongly based on the assumption that an AE needs to manage not only its internal behaviour but also the outside interactions [6]. Such interactions shall mostly translate into the exchange of some relevant signals and messages with other AEs, including the external world [6]. Consequently, the exchanged data is expected to be subject to being processed and issued by the internal logic driven by the objectives embedded into it, as defined by the system architect [6]. Given the existence of vertical, i.e. peering or sibling, and the horizontal, i.e. parental, relations, one may imagine a potentially three-dimensional grid of AEs attempting to maintain equilibrium yet fulfilling certain goal or goals at the same time. This, once again, brings about the reminiscence of the ant colony thus highlighting the very delicate difference between the notion of being autonomic and the notion of being able to reason through thinking. Ants are, in fact, separate organisms moving around together as a symbiotic group which is conceptually quite similar to yet another example of an increased human body temperature that cannot be explicitly driven by the thinking organ, i.e. the brain, but, instead, is controlled by the autonomic behaviour of different organs.

## 2.5   Agent Systems and Autonomic Entities

As argued in the pioneering work on Autonomic Computing this very concept is claimed to be rather deeply rooted in the theory of agent systems, since autonomy, proactivity, and goal-directed interactivity are the distinguishing characteristics of software agents [6]. What is more, the aforementioned concept of self-management spans not only over single-agent and multi-agent systems, but it also encompasses the rationale behind Service Oriented Architecture (SOA). The above is advocated for on the basis of the comparison between the following definitions referring to both the autonomic computing systems and software agents, respectively, i.e. "computing systems that can manage themselves given high-level objectives from administrators" as opposed to "an encapsulated computer system, situated in some environment and capable of flexible, autonomous action in that environment in order to meet its design objectives". In fact, both definitions appear to go hand-in-hand and the similarity is obvious, especially that they are cited by undoubtedly one of the milestone publications in the field of autonomic computing, i.e. [6]. Reading into the details one should note, however, that the definition of a software agent clearly mentions the notion of being autonomous but not autonomic. While this might be perceived as a diminishable detail at first sight, after a more thorough analysis it, unfortunately, no longer appears to be so.

More specifically, analysing the issue from a linguistic perspective, the word autonomous appears to have two main connotations of relevance to the argument. The definitions may be, in fact, derived immediately from the entries provided by the leading dictionaries which classify the notion of being autonomous as having the ability to work and make decisions by itself without any help from anyone else, in other words, independently [11], or making one's decisions on one's own rather than being influenced by somebody else [3].[6] First of all, the quality of being autonomous may be then attributed to a system which is of a stand-alone type in the sense that it is self-sufficient and, thus, may operate on its own, without any need for external orchestration, i.e. as a separate entity. Most obviously, the presented perception does not necessarily need to impose the full semantic meaning of autonomics. Secondly, one may think more of a cognitive flavour where the system is autonomous in the sense that is exposes, somewhat, a further advanced quality of being able to reason. Such a quality could manifest itself through the ability to make decisions following some hidden logic, as if the said system was steered by a brain-like device. Quite not surprisingly, also this connotation is certainly not very fortunate as autonomics detaches the features of an Autonomic Nervous System from the learned decisions of the brain it is linked to.

What is more, maybe even a bit unexpectedly, automation of a relevant form and type appears to have been also deployed for the needs of the exploration of the outer space and, consequently, even in that very field one may come across a definite distinction between the notion of autonomics and autonomy. In fact, it is claimed that "while autonomy supports cost-effective accomplishment of mission goals, autonomicity supports survivability of remote mission assets, especially when tending by humans is not feasible" [14]. One should note, however, that in spite of being highly useful, the above citation brings about yet another issue, this time related to the very word "autonomicity", which does not seem to exist in the major dictionaries, if in any at all. This term is currently rather being coined, not only in the cited publication but also in the specifications released by Industry Specification Group on Autonomic network engineering for the self-managing Future Internet (ISG AFI), functioning under the auspices of the European Telecommunications Standards Institute (ETSI).[7] Both expressions mean automation but here autonomy appears to pertain more to the lack of human control, while autonomics seems to refer to the employment of the principles behind the functioning of the Autonomic Nervous System.

This shows very clearly that even though there is a justified temptation to put both autonomic and agent-driven systems under the very same umbrella, a certain dose of prudence is necessary to avoid any unintended introduction of an unnecessary bias related to the proper understanding of the term "autonomics." What is more, even assuming that there could exist a sufficient dose of correspondence between the two concepts manifesting itself through the employment of individual self-

---

[6]The connotations outlined by the author come more from relevant academic and industrial discussions, and especially those related to the author's standardisation activity within Industry Specification Group on Autonomic network engineering for the self-managing Future Internet (ISG AFI) of the European Telecommunications Standards Institute.

[7]Unfortunately, according to the author's observations, even though "autonomicity" gains more and more recognition among the experts seeking for the proper expression of their intended meaning, this term appears not to be very well received by the native English language speakers and should be used rather carefully, if at all.

managing Decision Making Elements (DMEs), an autonomic system should be rather analysed from the perspective of Multi-Agent Systems (MASs), as the majority of autonomic systems are composed of multiple sub-systems or services while agent systems comprise multiple agents [1]. This is, in fact, where the Service Oriented Architecture (SOA) related context comes, very neatly, step-by-step, into the global picture of the synergy between the above-mentioned technologies of Autonomic Computing and Multi-Agent Systems. Going further, the autonomic DMEs are claimed to very much resemble software agents in the sense that the latter similarly act on the basis of both the monitoring information obtained from sensors and the imposed policies [1]. Obviously, even though there really appear to exist clear and tight links between both the concepts, one needs to be careful not to warp the sense of autonomic computing by not attributing to autonomics what does not really belong with it.

## 2.6  Convergence and Self-Awareness

Originally, the process of network management was virtually entirely based on the human-in-the-loop style [4]. The human role was, in fact, exposed to so high an extent that any automation in today's understanding, i.e. organised on a global scale, appeared out of the question or, at least, unattainable, mostly because of the technological obstacles, not to even mention the related deficiency in highly complex architectural developments. This was chiefly changed with the advent of advanced computing systems as devised and introduced by the key stakeholders in the computer market [12]. Consequently, relatively soon after, one could have observed not only a steady but, in fact, an exponential, increase in the incorporation and adoption of the more and more ubiquitous software-based components and entities into the very world of networking. Interestingly, it is actually claimed that should aircraft improve at the same pace as computers, "transatlantic flights would take no more than a few minutes and cost no more than a few dollars" [8].

In fact, as already indicated, the advancement in global convergence between the worlds of computing and networking has most recently reached its apogee, in the positively constructive meaning, and it is becoming more and more difficult to tell the two technological fields apart. The still some years ago rather vivid borders between or among various computer systems connected by telecommunications networks seem to have disappeared and, thus, the hybrid solution may be referred to as, for example, an Autonomic Networked Computing System (ANCS) [13], in order to somewhat artificially emphasise the currently rather passé distinctiveness of both elements, on the one hand, while clearly indicating the actually existing ultimate closeness calling for both the constituents to be perceived as one entity, on the other hand. In fact, it transpires that one of the key drivers for such a high level of convergence is the need of an autonomic networked computing system to be self-contained in the sense of being capable of exposing the ability to behave in a self-aware manner.

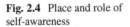
**Fig. 2.4** Place and role of
self-awareness

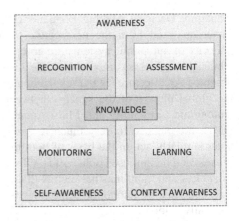

Self-awareness, in particular, goes hand-in-hand with autonomics, as it assumes
the exploitation of the acquired knowledge for the "understanding" of the system
status change along with the pertinent implications [15]. Following the classification
contained in Fig. 2.4, one may notice, however, that self-awareness in not really
a stand-alone feature of an autonomic system, but it is rather complemented by
the concept of context awareness. From such a perspective, the context awareness may be defined as the knowledge of a system of how to interact with its
surrounding environment through communication and negotiation for the purposes
of being able to predict the forthcoming situational states and changes in advance.
Most importantly, both self-awareness and context awareness revolve around the
above-mentioned focal component denoted as knowledge and are both based on
two functional entities, i.e. recognition and monitoring, as well as learning and
assessment, respectively [15].

In this respect, the task of recognition is defined to correspond to the exploitation
of knowledge for the purposes of tracking changes, while monitoring, most
naturally, provides the data necessary for building such knowledge by means
of collecting, aggregating, and processing the acquired information [15]. The
assessment, in turn, is claimed to be mostly related to testing hypotheses and
identifying situational schemata while being responsible for the triggering of
learning processes consisting in the formulation of new situational schemata and
keeping track of the system evolution history [15]. Based on the cited reference
literature one may conclude that there seems to be much more to self-awareness than
plain autonomics. In other words, as already indicated, the meaning of autonomics
should not be confused with cognition and reasoning, however, while self-awareness
clearly involves the processes of learning, it may imply a bit more than simple
monitoring for a purely mechanical context recognition.

## 2.7 Conclusion

In this chapter the rationale behind the concept of autonomic computing and its convergence with modern networked systems was presented. To this end an extensive conceptual analysis was carried out to provide the most comprehensive overview of today's status and role of autonomics. In particular, the general vision and the state-of-the-art in the field of autonomic computer system design was introduced on the basis of the adaptation of the mechanisms driving the behaviour of human Autonomic Nervous System. This involved the discussion of certain aspects of self-configuration, self-optimisation, self-healing, and self-protection, as the chief constituents of the device of self-management. Following, the relevant architectural assumptions and variations were analysed and, then, made subject to the argument regarding the complementary nature of autonomics and agent systems. Finally, the question of convergence between computer and networked systems was investigated to lay the ground for the discussion of the role of self-awareness of the fused architecture of an Autonomic Networked Computing System. Based on this, the novel concept of Autonomic Cooperative System Architectural Model (ACSAM) will be outlined in the next chapter.

## References

1. Brazier, F. M. T., Kephart, J. O., Van Dyke Parunak, H., & Huhns, M. N. (2009) Agents and Service-oriented computing for autonomic computing: A research agenda. *IEEE Internet Computing, 13*(3), 82–87.
2. Chaparadza, R., Papavassiliou, S., Kastrinogiannis, T., Vigoureux, M., Dotaro, E., Davy, K. A., et al. (2009) Creating a viable evolution path towards self-managing future internet via a standardizable reference model for autonomic network engineering. In: G. Tselentis, J. Domingue, A. Galis, A. Gavras, D. Hausheer, S. Krco, V. Lotz, & T. Zahariadis (Eds.) *Towards the future internet: A European research perspective.* Amsterdam: IOS Press. ISBN: 978-1-60750-007-0 (Also published at the Future Internet Assembly 2009 in Prague).
3. Collins Cobuild (1997). *Collins Cobuild english dictionary.* New York: HarperCollins.
4. Herrmann, K., Muhl, G., & Geihs, K. (2005) Self management: The solution to complexity or just another problem?. *IEEE Distributed Systems Online, 6*(1), 1–17.
5. Hinchey, M. G., & Sterritt, R. (2006) Self-managing software. *IEEE Computer, 39*(2), 107–109.
6. Kephart, J. O., & Chess, D. M. (2003) The vision of autonomic computing. *IEEE Computer, 36*(1), 41–50.
7. Kephart, J. O., & Das, R. (2007) Achieving self-management via utility functions. *IEEE Internet Computing, 11*(1), 40–48.
8. Mainsah, E. (2002) Autonomic computing: The next era of computing. *Electronics and Communication Engineering Journal 14*(1), 2–3. .
9. Movahedi, Z., Ayari M., Langar R., & Pujolle, G. (2012) A survey of autonomic network architectures and evaluation criteria. *IEEE Communications Surveys and Tutorials, 14*(2), 464–490.
10. Paulson, L. D. (2002) Computer system, heal thyself. *IEEE Computer, 35*(8), 20–22.
11. Pearson Education Limited (2003). *Longman dictionary of contemporary english.* Harlow: Pearson Education Limited, 2003.

12. Pescovitz, D. (2002) Helping computers help themselves. *IEEE Spectrum, 39*(9), 49–53.
13. Phan, C.-V. (2009) Autonomic computing and networking. In *Formal aspects of self-\* in autonomic networked computing systems* (pp. 381–410). New York: Springer
14. Truszkowski, W. F., Hinchey, M. G., Rash, J. L., & Rouff, C. A. (2006) Autonomous and autonomic systems: A paradigm for future space exploration missions. *IEEE Transactions on Systems, Man, and Cybernetics Part C (IEEE Transactions on Human-Machine Systems), 36*(3), 279–291.
15. Vassev, E., & Hinchey, M. (2010) The challenge of developing autonomic systems. *IEEE Computer, 43*(12), 93–96.
16. Wódczak, M. (2011, November). Resilience aspects of autonomic cooperative communications in context of cloud networking. In *IEEE First Symposium on Network Cloud Computing and Applications*. Toulouse, France, pp. 21–23.
17. Wódczak, M., Meriem, T. B., Radier, B., Chaparadza, R., Quinn, K., Kielthy, J., et al. (2011) Standardizing a reference model and autonomic network architectures for the self-managing future internet. *IEEE Network, 25*(6), 50–56.
18. Yixin, D., Hellerstein, J. L., Parekh, S., Griffith, R., Kaiser, G. E., & Phung, D. (2005) A control theory foundation for self-managing computing systems. *IEEE Journal on Selected Areas in Communications, 23*(12), 2213–2222.

# Chapter 3
# Autonomic Cooperative System Architecture

## 3.1 Introduction

Following the opening analysis of the increasingly convergent world of autonomic computing and networking, which intended to provide a comprehensive and consistent explanation of today's role and place of autonomics, this chapter aims much more to investigate and outline certain relevant state-of-the-art architectural advancements in this very field in order to pave the ground for the introduction of the idea of Autonomic Cooperative System Architectural Model (ACSAM). In fact, first of all, the concept of Autonomic Cooperative System Architectural Model is outlined with special emphasis on the aspects related to novelty with regard to the current trends. To this end, the Generic Autonomic Network Architecture is taken as an example Reference Architecture and is overviewed as the baseline solution for the further development to be outlined in the remainder of this book. In this respect, a special attention is paid to the notion of Autonomic Control Loops (ACLs) operating on various levels of abstraction along with the explanation of their role when perceived bottom-up, i.e. down from the protocol level, through the function and node ones, up to the network level. As a result, the aforementioned Autonomic Cooperative System Architectural Model is outlined with the inclusion of its key components of ACNP and ACB, to be further analysed in the following chapters. In particular, at this stage the reader is already familiarised with the key concept of Autonomic Cooperative Node (ACN) being, in fact, the main enabler for the instantiation of the said ACB.

## 3.2 Concept and Novelty

This book aims to investigate and present the theoretical and practical aspects of enhancing the general concept of Autonomic Networked Computing System (ANCS) with the new notion of Autonomic Cooperative Behaviour (ACB). As

M. Wódczak, *Autonomic Computing Enabled Cooperative Networked Design*,
SpringerBriefs in Computer Science, DOI 10.1007/978-1-4939-0764-9_3,
© The Author(s) 2014

already indicated in the previous chapter, the inherent feature of the biology and nature inspired autonomic computing translates, in fact, into self-management which consists in the ability of the related networked computing system to self-configure, self-optimise, self-heal, and self-protect without any explicit need for external human intervention [1, 14]. At the same time the idea of instantiating cooperation among distributed nodes of such a networked system assumes that cooperative data processing may increase the overall system robustness and dependability [18]. Given the above assumption, the main objective is to provide a design of a holistic distributed Autonomic Cooperative System Architectural Model (ACSAM) encompassing a relevantly tailored Autonomic Cooperative Networking Protocol (ACNP), where the architectural entities, as well as the network nodes they are orchestrating, may express Autonomic Cooperative Behaviour, either because they are requested or choose themselves to do so. There may arise a potential danger, however, as, quite interestingly, when attempted to be treated jointly, both the terms of autonomics and cooperation could be also perceived as, somewhat, mutually exclusive. In other words, if a given set of cooperating nodes acts as a unified entity then its Autonomic Cooperative Behaviour may be expected to be atomic in the sense that there should not be contradiction between any two or more nodes constituting such a group. On the other hand, however, should not the said Autonomic Cooperative Behaviour be atomic, as it is expected to be the case in reality, the constituting nodes may express egoistic tendencies,[1] resulting from disjoint policies imposed on them either internally or externally.

In fact, the presented concept stems from an interdisciplinary research field of mapping the rationale behind the autonomic functioning of a living organism onto a networked computing system [15]. This is where a novel concept of instantiating and trading off Autonomic Cooperative Behaviour for increased system resilience and dependability is introduced and applied. Most obviously, a direct correspondence between nature and computer systems does not really exist and the extent to which the two may go hand-in-hand is highly dependant on the assumed modelling principles. Therefore, it is necessary to devise such a distributed Autonomic Cooperative System Architectural Model that would guarantee the possibility for autonomics and cooperation to interact together efficiently enough to provide the predicted increased stability and dependability of the resulting system.[2] From the research perspective, thanks to the required incorporation of autonomics, such an approach will help in obtaining a better understanding of the processes going on in networked cooperative systems, where an insufficiently thoughtful design could rather adversely influence the said overall system stability, and,

---

[1] In this sense, egoistic tendencies not necessarily need to be intentional or deliberate. Given the rationale behind autonomic system functioning, they should be rather expected to result from an improper design. In general, however, such a problem could be more natural for Artificial Intelligence (AI) orientated approaches.

[2] In general, this is expected to be feasible, as long as the relevant architectural entities ensure that Autonomic Cooperative Behaviour is free of the above-mentioned egoistic tendencies.

thus, its related resilience and dependability. In fact, the concept of Autonomic Cooperative System Architectural Model goes way beyond the current developments in the field of autonomic system design, as it incorporates the notion of Autonomic Cooperative Behaviour through the use of a properly tailored Autonomic Cooperative Networking Protocol. Thus far, most of the effort towards seeking innovation within the domain of autonomics has been based on a most obviously silent assumption that a networked computer system should follow the rationale behind the functioning of an Autonomic Nervous System, where different organs operating by themselves naturally entangle in a "constructive" cooperation[3] enabled by the control information coming from this very Autonomic Nervous System. Such an approach could be fully justified if cooperation solely meant information exchange but not a joint action. As there may exist the previously indicated dose of contradiction between autonomics and cooperation, there is a need for the provision of an unprecedented and balanced solution capitalising on the joint advantages of the two.

## 3.3   Reference Generic Autonomic Network Architecture

In order for the workings of the Autonomic Cooperative System Architectural Model to be outlined, first it is necessary to introduce the Generic Autonomic Network Architecture (GANA) reference model [3, 17].[4,5] Given the context of Autonomic Computing (AC), as introduced in Chap. 2, Autonomic Networking (AN) emerged soon after its predecessor, thus becoming one of the most promising approaches towards the instantiation of the self-managing networked system of the future, and the Future Internet in particular [4]. As already signalled, the architecture of reference was devised under the name of Generic Autonomic Network Architecture and with the objective of being fully reflective of the notion of autonomics by becoming clearly distinctive from the device of cognition or the ability of acting autonomously. One should note, however, that, in general, the said distinction does not exclude the cognitive and autonomous flavour but, instead, it attempts to achieve a well-structured categorisation of all the pertinent and related

---

[3]In this sense, potentially, the notion of cooperation rather translates into the supportive class which, at least in the context of networked systems, implies more the information exchange rather than simultaneous and joint data processing, as further explained in Sect. 4.2.

[4]In fact, the author of this book is one of the contributors to and co-authors of the final version of the GANA Reference Architecture, as he was involved in the European Union Integrated Project EU FP7 EFIPSANS (Exposing the Features in IP version Six protocols that can be exploited/extended for the purposes of designing/building Autonomic Networks and Services), and, since then, has continued the relevant work under the auspices of the European Telecommunications Standards Institute (ETSI) as a Vice-Chairman and Rapporteur of the Industry Specification Group (ISG) on Autonomic network engineering for the self-managing Future Internet (AFI).

[5]For further reading the reader is also referred to [2, 10].

notions thereof, so that an autonomic system could be precisely characterised by
the capability of exercising the task of self-management without a specific need
for any external intervention on the side of a human administrator, for computing
systems, or operator, for networked systems [9].[6] Given the already indicated
convergence between computing and networking, however, any strict distinction
between administrator and operator is becoming rather artificial [5, 11].

In fact, one of the key inherent features of Autonomic Networking is the need
for continuous monitoring so that a networked system is able to self-manage
according to the internally or externally imposed policies while taking into account
additional information, such as the one related to root causes and incidents, the
use of which may substantially improve the overall system dependability and
resilience[7] through proper fault-management [12]. The aforementioned factors are
particularly important for Mobile Ad-hoc NETwork (MANET) related scenarios,
which depending on the set-up, might be characterised by a very dynamically
changing topology affecting the ability of networked nodes to efficiently express
Autonomic Cooperative Behaviour. In other words, from a general viewpoint, such
an Autonomic Networking should imitate the behaviour of a living organism's
autonomic nervous system in terms of being continually driven by a substantial
number of processes, similarly to the Autonomic Nervous System, i.e. running
on their own but remaining in close correlation without any specific need for
orchestration form a central entity for most of the time of operation. To map
such a concept onto an Autonomic Networked Computing System it is necessary
to apply specific network engineering mechanisms which are currently being
transferred from a pre-standardisation into the standardisation phase within the
European Telecommunications Standards Institute, and the Industry Specification
Group on Autonomic network engineering for the self-managing Future Internet, in
particular [17]. The Generic Autonomic Network Architecture reference model, as
presented in Fig. 3.1, advocates for a holistic approach so that not only distinct
networked nodes are supposed to express Autonomic Behaviour (AB) but the
distributed system is expected to function autonomically as a whole.

Following, it is claimed that such a networked system should monitor itself
in a continuously operating Autonomic Control Loop (ACL) or, rather, apply
a whole plethora of ACLs functioning at a different pace while being located
on different abstraction levels. In fact, there are four distinct abstraction levels
distinguishable spanning up from the network, through the node and function, down
to the protocol one,[8] interacting between themselves both top-down and bottom-up

---

[6]For the further explanation of the discussed distinction the reader is referred directly to the
argument contained in Sect. 2.5.

[7]Dependability, understood as the ability of a system to be trusted to perform what one needs or
expects [13], is rather the term of computing. In networking, however, another capability exists,
usually referred to as resilience and tightly connected with survivability which pertains much more
to system durability. This way or another, it appears that dependability may be expressed as a
function of resilience.

[8]The precise role of the abstraction levels will be further elaborated in Sect. 3.4.

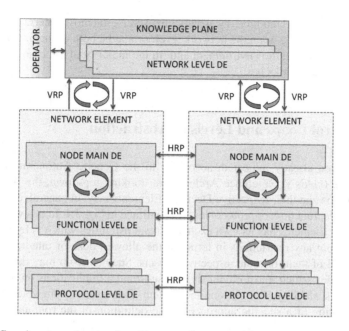

**Fig. 3.1** Generic autonomic network architecture reference model

through Vertical Reference Points (VRPs) over control loops in one dimension, as well as through Horizontal Reference Points (HRPs) in the other dimension. It is of prime importance that the said system express the ability to align its currently ongoing operation with the requirements arising from such monitoring data or, simply, imposed by presumably changing external and internal policies on all the above-mentioned abstraction levels. In other words, distinct networked nodes of the baseline Generic Autonomic Network Architecture should express Autonomic Behaviour but, in specific cases, the relevant decisions may need to be taken at the network level.[9] As a result, in certain circumstances, the freedom of a Decision Element (DE) to make a decision based just on the available information can be limited by directions given by a higher level DE, as outlined in Fig. 3.1. This is where the knowledge plane, complementary to the network level, comes into the picture [6]. Going further, clearly, the decisions might need to be taken at the network level in order to make it feasible for the networked system to perform tasks of a global scope, for example, as a result of the highest priority indication coming from the system administrator or operator. At the same time certain local-scope arrangements, such as the yet to be introduced Autonomic Cooperative Behaviour between or among networked nodes, may be carried out smoothly and without any interruption, most obviously as long as any of the imposed system rules and policies

---

[9]As it will be shown in Sect. 3.4, the network level may only exist conceptually and it is formed by elevated nodes inherently belonging to the node level at most.

are not to be violated. Undoubtedly, whether to exercise the most generic Autonomic Behaviour on the node or on the network level, or maybe both of them, depends on the character of a specific environment and, in the majority of the cases, usually a trade-off approach works best.

## 3.4   Control Loops and Levels of Abstraction

As it has been already indicated, according to the Generic Autonomic Network Architecture (GANA) Reference Architecture, looking top-down, the Autonomic Control Loops and their respective Decision Elements may, in general, exist on the network, node, function, or protocol level, as outlined in Fig. 3.1. In this way each of the Decision Elements has its own exclusive responsibilities which is by no means intended to put any restrictions in terms of the allowed dose of interaction going on among all of them or their respective subsets. Such a set-up may then become highly complex which, most obviously, has substantial implications on the overall stability and scalability of an Autonomic System. This issue is somewhat addressed by the adoption of a specific approach to the definition of the role and scope of theAutonomic Control Loops located on the aforementioned levels.[10] In particular, when viewed from the bottom-up perspective, the multi-tier concept of Generic Autonomic Network Architecture makes a very correct impression of being highly hierarchical. In other words, the higher the level, the wider the scope of a given Decision Element and the Autonomic Control Loop it is running, which means that its control may span over and oversee many lower level Decision Elements, as well as their respective ACLs. What is more, in general, the higher the level is, the slower the pace at which a given Autonomic Control Loop is running. This way the Autonomic System is expected to be scalable, as it always allows for the inclusion of such "parent" Decision Elements on a specific level to encompass and orchestrate the behaviour of their "child" Decision Elements[11] one level below. Complementary to scalability, in turn, is the pace changing with level, being expected to help in guaranteeing the expectedly increased degree of stability. All four levels will be briefly characterised in the following paragraph on the basis of the latest ETSI group specification co-authored by the author of this book [8], while more specific architectural extensions will be proposed in Chap. 6.

As depicted in Fig. 3.2, the Autonomic Control Loop of the lowest, protocol level is steered by the protocol level Decision Element which orchestrates the Managed

---

[10]In the GANA specification the Autonomic Control Loops are referred to as Hierarchical Control Loops.

[11]One should note, however, that in the case of a protocol level DE there is no lower level DE and, instead, the Managed Entity assumes directly the form of a managed resource, usually being a relevant protocol. On the other hand, such a protocol could contain its own internal Autonomic Control Loops, yet the concept of Generic Autonomic Network Architecture does not really advocate for the introduction of protocol intrinsic ACLs for complexity related reasons.

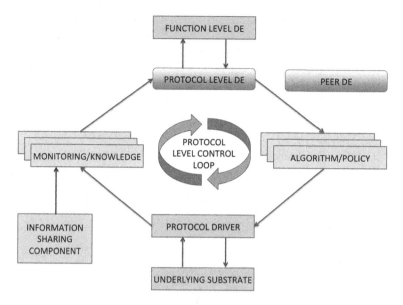

**Fig. 3.2** Protocol level autonomic control loop

Entity in the form of the protocol driver interfacing with a specific protocol of the Open Systems Interconnection (OSI) or Transmission Control Protocol/Internet Protocol (TCP/IP) model, for example. In particular, the said protocols may be of a modular or monolithic nature, potentially including their own internal Autonomic Control Loop [8]. One should note, however, that according to the GANA Reference Architecture it is not recommended to deploy ACLs within protocols which, instead, should be kept simple and rather designed to interface efficiently with GANA itself. It is claimed that protocol intrinsic ACLs could unnecessarily make Generic Autonomic Network Architecture prone to stability issues as the current extent of hierarchical complexity is already sufficiently high. Immediately above the described protocol level, there is the function level pertaining rather to the so-called abstract network layer functions than the protocols themselves, as outlined in Fig. 3.3. The notion of such a function encompasses then the general functionality of routing or mobility management, for example [8]. As such, the role of the function level translates more into a proper configuration of specific protocols through the mechanism of Autonomic Control Loops intended to facilitate the process of event monitoring and tracking.

Following, the two key levels of a wider scope are coming towards the top of the Generic Autonomic Network Architecture Reference Architecture. The node level may be, in fact, perceived as the highest physical entity of its sort as the network level is more of a conceptual or even abstract nature. In particular, being located right above the function level, the node level pertains to the system represented by a networked node as a whole. Such a privileged position means that, on the one hand, the node level DE, as outlined in Fig. 3.4, has direct access to the requirements

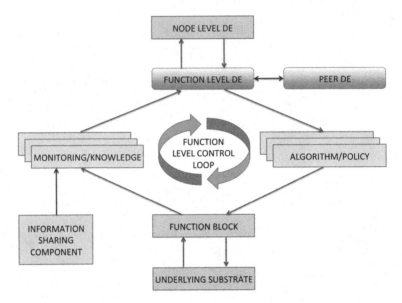

**Fig. 3.3** Function level autonomic control loop

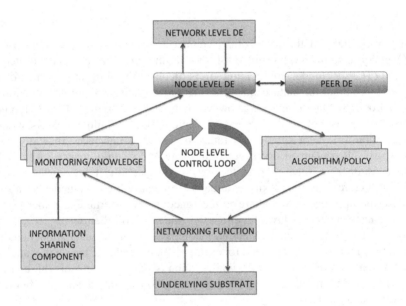

**Fig. 3.4** Node level autonomic control loop

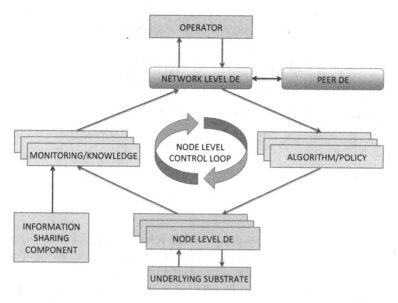

**Fig. 3.5** Network level autonomic control loop

exposed by the function level DEs and, on the other hand, it has access to all the necessary information related to the system priorities of the node level itself [8]. What is more, it takes all the relevant directions immediately from the network level DE making it altogether a kind of a hub being responsible for the entire node. Going further, as there is no physical device of a network, it is rather formed by purposely elevated nodes characterised by certain extended capabilities. Especially in mobile networks, such a capability may translate in an improved durability in terms of a given node being equipped with a much more capacious battery. The need for such an assumption becomes even more conspicuous given the fact that there may be one network level DE only, as presented in Fig. 3.5. Most obviously, such a Decision Element may be fairly complicated due to its most elevated role and, thus, its core functionality should be made modular, as originally indicated in Fig. 3.1. This way the centralisation may contain certain dose of being distributed for optimisation reasons. There is also another possibility, where a fully distributed solution is implemented but in such a case those are network level Decision Elements to be entitled to make all the global scope decisions in a cooperative manner [8].

## 3.5  Autonomic Cooperative System Architectural Model

Following the introduction of the Generic Autonomic Network Architecture, this section is intended to lay the ground for the proposed solution of Autonomic Cooperative System Architectural Model (ACSAM) to be detailed in the following chapters. As depicted in Fig. 3.6, the Autonomic Cooperative System Architectural

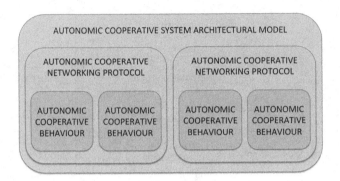

**Fig. 3.6** Autonomic cooperative system architectural model

Model is based on a theoretical design of the relevant architectural components comprising the Autonomic Cooperative Behaviour and the Autonomic Cooperative Networking Protocol, in particular, while being orthogonal to the concept of the Autonomic Cooperative Node, to be detailed in next section, with its respective Decision Making Elements (DMEs).[12] From the perspective of the Open Systems Interconnection (OSI) Reference Model (RM), a special emphasis is put on the network layer allowing for physical interactions among the distributed ACNs. In particular, however, keeping in mind the context of the human Autonomic Nervous System, as such, organs do not cooperate per se, while network nodes may and should in order to guarantee the desired resilience and dependability of a self-healing distributed networked system [7]. Therefore, given all the advantages of today's state-of-the-art developments, they are, most clearly, becoming obsolete and it is necessary to accommodate the new dimension advocated for by the notion of Autonomic Cooperative Behaviour. Due to a very high complexity of the analysed distributed system, a simulation analysis will be carried out with the use of a proprietary, Java programming language based, simulation environment allowing for a highly modular multi-threaded implementation and simulation of the proposed concepts, as presented in detail in Chap. 7.

Analysing various scenarios of applicability, a full ability to exercise Autonomic Cooperative Behaviour at the node level might be of prime importance, for example, for Mobile Ad-hoc NETworks, composed of the end user equipment meaning that it is the user to cover the cost and not the service provider. Quite the contrary, one would probably emphasise the network level much more, when the access devices, such as Radio Access Points (RAPs), Relay Nodes (RNs), or Base Stations (BSs), deployed by a specific network operator to form the Radio Access Network (RAN), are concerned. Ideally, the network should be autonomic and, at the same time,

---

[12] A Decision Making Element should be perceived as a special form of a Decision Making Entity (DME), which, in fact, carries the same acronym, thus potentially creating some unintended confusion.

the Autonomic Cooperative Behaviour of distinct networked nodes should not be affected. It means that in case there is a need for a Mobile Ad-hoc NETwork to request a networked node to act as a cooperating router that node might be offered certain incentive, such as, for example, free-of-charge access to service, playing not only the role of an incentive, but also intended to compensate for quicker battery drainage, as well as any potential security threats. Such threats are envisioned to be arising from the fact that granting somebody else's device cooperative access to one's networked device may potentially induce an unwanted installation of malicious software. Hard to tackle as it may seem, one might still attempt to consider the introduction of certain mechanisms for motivating the networked nodes, and in fact the end users, to trade their level of being autonomic for certain benefits and incentives in order to make it possible for the whole group of networked nodes to meet the predefined goals. In other words, an autonomic network formed of autonomic components should be then able to carry out clear internal negotiations in order to reach a common agreement. GANA assumes this to be done through cooperative interactions among DEs so that the resulting service is more likely to be guaranteed in situations where typically it would be very difficult or even impossible to be handled.

## 3.6 Autonomic Cooperative Node

The instantiation of Autonomic Cooperative Behaviour, being one of the core functionalities of the Autonomic Cooperative System Architectural Model, requires the introduction of certain extensions to the baseline Generic Autonomic Network Architecture. While such extensions will be the main theme of the remainder of this book, one of the key concepts needs to be introduced at this point already. The said concept pertains to the extension of the GANA AN to a more flexible structure of the Autonomic Cooperative Node (ACN) intended to provide additional gain in terms of resilience and dependability. In fact, one of the key characteristics of ASs is the ability to perform the not always orthogonally composed task of self-discovery which may comprise, for example, service discovery, topology discovery, fault discovery, etc. It is expected that cooperative composition of such components may only further enhance the effectiveness of the autonomic networked system configuration and its overall performance. However, in order to accommodate such a functionality in the most proper and effective manner it is primarily assumed that the role of the classic Autonomic Node should by enhanced with the notion of Autonomic Cooperative Behaviour in such a way that any ACN is always able to downgrade to the base level of AN without a penalty to the operation of the Autonomic System. In other words, ACN is intended to provide elevated functionality helping the legacy AS to become more resilient and dependable, as long as the functioning of other entities remains intact.

The proposed concept of Autonomic Cooperative Node is outlined in Fig. 3.7, where some additional Decision Elements of relevance are displayed to be further

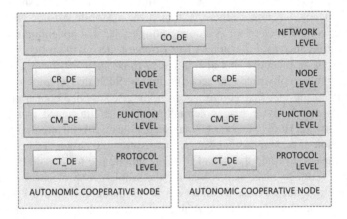

**Fig. 3.7** Autonomic cooperative node

elaborated on in the following chapters. For the sake of introduction, however, it is necessary to underline that the existence and the scope of the aforementioned four levels of GANA RA remain conceptually unchanged [18]. The novelty consists rather in the introduction of the ACN itself along with all its pertinent key DEs. In particular, starting from the protocol level, there is a modified Cooperative Transmission Decision Element CT_DE deployed which is responsible for the interactions with the routines of the Optimised Link State Routing (OLSR) protocol taking care of the integration of cooperative transmission into the Multi-Point Relay (MPR) selection heuristics. However, in the case of this book, following the GANA assumption related to protocol simplicity, certain logic previously additionally embedded in the OLSR protocol is now elevated to the function level, where an entirely new Cooperation Management Decision Element CM_DE is located, quite differently comparing to the original solution [18]. The main responsibility of CM_DE is to take over, assume, and extend the previously internal task of the modified Optimised Link State Routing protocol, featuring the Routing information Enhanced Algorithm for Cooperative

Transmission (REACT) [16], which consisted in assigning nodes to Virtual Antenna Arrays (VAAs) and, thus, instantiating Distributed Spatio-Temporal Block Coding (DSTBC) between or among the nodes exposing Autonomic Cooperative Behaviour. Moving up the GANA abstraction levels, the node level contributes with the inclusion of the so necessary resilience and dependability through the introduction of the Cooperative Re-Routing Decision Element CR_DE. This DE, having access to some other DEs, such as the Resilience and Survivability Decision Element RS_DE and its related Fault Management Decision Element FM_DE, both being able to jointly control the symptoms suggesting that a failure may be imminent and reacting appropriately, may trigger the relevant cooperative re-routing procedure well in advance and, thus, guarantee service continuity. Last but not least is the new Cooperation Orchestration Decision Element CO_DE being responsible for overseeing the overall Autonomic Cooperative Behaviour related situation of the Autonomic System from the highest, network-level perspective, and, orchestrating various ACB accordingly.

## 3.7 Conclusion

In this chapter, the opening analysis of the convergence between autonomic computing and networking was complemented with the investigation of the state-of-the-art concept of Generic Autonomic Network Architecture Reference Architecture. Based on this the idea of Autonomic Cooperative System Architectural Model (ACSAM) was introduced and special emphasis was placed on the aspects related to the proposed novelty in the context of the nowadays' trends. A special attention was paid to the explanation of the role of Autonomic Control Loops together with their respective levels of abstraction presented bottom-up, i.e. from the protocol, through the function and node, up to the network level. Once the ground has been settled, the scope of the Autonomic Cooperative System Architectural Model was presented, including its key components of ACNP and ACB, to undergo further detailed analysis in the following chapters. Given its key role, the key concept of Autonomic Cooperative Node (ACN) was already introduced where the target Decision Elements were located and their general role briefly described, as ACNs should be perceived as the main enablers for the instantiation of the notion of Autonomic Cooperative Behaviour to be introduced in next chapter.

## References

1. Bicocchi, N. & Zambonelli, F. (2007). Autonomic communication learns from nature. *IEEE Potentials*, 26(6), 42–46.
2. Bouabene, G., Jelger, C., Tschudin, C., Schmid, S., Keller, A., & May, M. (2010). The Autonomic Network Architecture (ANA). *IEEE Journal on Selected Areas in Communications*, 28(1), 4–14.
3. Chaparadza, R. (2008). Requirements for a Generic Autonomic Network Architecture (GANA), suitable for Standardizable Autonomic Behaviour Specifications of Decision-Making-Elements (DMEs) for Diverse Networking Environments. *International Engineering Consortium (IEC) in the Annual Review of Com., 61*
4. Chaparadza, R., Papavassiliou, S., Kastrinogiannis, T., Vigoureux, M., Dotaro, E., Davy, A., et al. (2009). Creating a viable evolution path towards self-managing future internet via a standardizable reference model for autonomic network engineering. G. Tselentis, J. Domingue, A. Galis, A. Gavras, D. Hausheer, S. Krco, V. Lotz, & T. Zahariadis (Eds.) *Chapter in the book: "Towards the Future Internet - A European Research Perspective*, IOS Press, ISBN: 978-1-60750-007-0. Also published at the Future Internet Assembly 2009 in Prague.
5. Cheng, Y., Leon-Garcia, A., & Foster, I. (2008). Toward an autonomic service management framework: a Holistic vision of SOA, AON, and autonomic computing. *IEEE Communications Magazine*, 46(5), 138–146.

6. Clark, D. D., Partridge, C., Ramming, J. C., & Wroclawski J. T. (2007). A knowledge plane for the internet. In *Proceedings of ACM SIGCOMM 2003*, Karlsruhe.
7. Dai, Y., Xiang, Y., Li, Y., Xing, L., & Zhang, G., (2011). Consequence oriented self-healing and autonomous diagnosis for highly reliable systems and software. *IEEE Transactions on Reliability*, *60*(2), 369–380.
8. ETSI GS AFI 002 V1.1.1. (2013). Autonomic network engineering for the self-managing future internet (AFI); generic autonomic network architecture (An architectural reference model for autonomic networking, cognitive networking and self-management). ETSI Group Specification, France.
9. Femminella, M., Francescangeli, R., Reali, G., Lee, J. W., & Schulzrinne H. (2011). An enabling platform for autonomic management of the future internet. *IEEE Network*, *25*(6), 24–32.
10. Greenberg, A., et al. (2005). A clean slate 4D approach to network control and management. *ACM SIGCOMM Computer Communication Review*, *35*(5), 41–54.
11. Jennings, B., van der Meer, S., Balasubramaniam, S., Botvich, D., Foghlu, M. O., Donnelly, W., et al. (2007). Towards autonomic management of communications networks. *IEEE Communications Magazine*, *45*(10), 112–121.
12. Liakopoulos, A., Zafeiropoulos, A., Polyrakis, A., Grammatikou, M., Gonzalez, J. M., Wódczak, M., et al. (2008). Monitoring issues for autonomic networks: the EFIPSANS vision. In *European Workshop on Mechanisms for the Future Internet*.
13. *Longman Dictionary of Contemporary English*. (2003). Pearson Education Limited.
14. Nakano, T. (2011). Biologically inspired network systems: a review and future prospects. *IEEE Transactions on Systems, Man, and Cybernetics Part C: Applications and Reviews (IEEE Transactions on Human-Machine Systems)*, *41*(5), 630–643.
15. Samaan, N., & Karmouch, A. (2009). Towards autonomic network management: an analysis of current and future research directions. *IEEE Communications Surveys and Tutorials*, *11*(3), 22–36.
16. Wódczak, M. (2007). Extended REACT - Routing information enhanced algorithm for cooperative transmission. In *16th IST Mobile & Wireless Communications Summit 2007*, Budapest, Hungary.
17. Wódczak, M., Meriem, T. B., Radier, B., Chaparadza, R., Quinn, K., Kielthy, J., et al. (2011) Standardizing a reference model and autonomic network architectures for the self-managing future internet. *IEEE Network*, *25*(6), 50–56.
18. Wódczak, M. (2012). *Autonomic cooperative networking*. New York: Springer.

# Chapter 4
# Autonomic Cooperative Behaviour

## 4.1 Introduction

Following the initial explanation of the rationale behind Autonomic Computing (AC) enabled cooperative networking in the opening chapter, extended with the details on the Autonomic Cooperative System Architectural Model (ACSAM), as proposed in the previous one, this chapter aims to introduce the very concept of Autonomic Cooperative Behaviour (ACB). As such, ACB constitutes the lowest level of the analysed three-tier architecture and is designed to be composed with the aid of creating Virtual Cooperative Sets (VCSs) and, then, orchestrated by the Autonomic Cooperative Networking Protocol, under the umbrella Autonomic Cooperative System Architectural Model. In fact, as regards the ACB itself, not only is it multi-faceted but also hardly definable. To account for its role and meaning, first of all the notion of cooperation is introduced to distinguish between and define collaborative and supportive protocols. Following, the Virtual Multiple Input Multiple Output (VMIMO) channel is described as the main enabler for an efficient instantiation of ACB, primarily through a properly tailored application of Distributed Spatio-Temporal Block Coding (DSTBC) among Autonomic Cooperative Nodes (ACNs). This phase should be perceived as the above-mentioned composition of ACB on the basis of Virtual Cooperative Sets stemming from the concept of Virtual Antenna Arrays (VAAs). The process of VCSs creation, in turn, is assumed to be integrated into and orchestrated by the Multi-Point Relay (MPR) station selection heuristics of the Optimised Link State Routing (OLSR) protocol.

## 4.2 Notion of Cooperation

Even though the notion of Autonomic Cooperative Behaviour (ACB) primarily stems from the concept of cooperative transmission, when scrutinised more thoroughly, it appears to be rather multi-faceted and, potentially, understandable in many different ways. In fact, as such, the term of cooperation may, at first, seem

M. Wódczak, *Autonomic Computing Enabled Cooperative Networked Design*,
SpringerBriefs in Computer Science, DOI 10.1007/978-1-4939-0764-9_4,
© The Author(s) 2014

intangible and neither easily quantifiable nor definable. However, when viewed from various high-level perspectives, the rationale behind its variety of forms appears to start becoming more and more justified. In particular, since cooperation among network nodes may take different shapes, cooperative transmission or relaying may be at most perceived as being merely one of its enablers. Attempting to generalise the notion of cooperation, one may even come to a conclusion that, in fact, any information exchange between, or among, potential Autonomic Cooperative Nodes (ACNs) may be also perceived as its instantiation. Going further, it transpires that there are two main classes of cooperation, the author of this book tries to distinguish by choosing the names of collaborative and supportive ones.[1] While a phrase such as "supportive cooperation" may be generally considered as more or less linguistically correct, the combination of "collaborative cooperation" calls immediately for the charge of tautology. Solely for this reason it is decided to rather subdivide cooperation into supportive protocols and collaborative protocols, altogether being the main constituents of and the enables for Autonomic Cooperative Behaviour, as depicted in Fig. 4.1.

**Fig. 4.1** Classification of cooperation methods

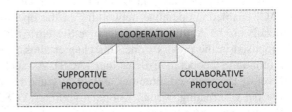

In fact the semantic fields of the words cooperation and collaboration overlap rather tightly. While cooperation is usually defined as a "joint operation or action", collaboration appears to expose a bit more the very "act of working with" other entities, thus being also known for its negative connotation [1]. This way a very thin borderline may be put between the two, making cooperation slightly more generic and collaboration slightly more specific, i.e. exactly as needed for the proposed classification. This way the class of collaborative protocols may encompass all the concepts stemming from the Link Layer cooperative transmission or relaying, where a group of networked nodes performs a joint action of, for example, processing the data signal broadcast from the Source Node (SN) towards the Destination Node (DN) by a group of cooperating Relay Nodes (RNs) according to a specific spatio-temporal block code matrix.[2] It is crucial to note that the joint action means performing the same activity, or a consistent part of such an activity in the case of a distributed processing of the columns of an orthogonal spatio-temporal block

---

[1]One should note, however, that such a naming structure may appear vague or inconsistent without taking into account the definitions to follow.

[2]The relevant spatio-temporal processing techniques will be introduced in Sect. 4.4, while the related cooperative transmission or relaying protocols will be outlined in Sect. 4.5.

code, at the same time, over a shared resource of the same radio channel in this very case, and intended to produce an immediate and tangible result. In other words the unity of action takes the precedence and the most important role here, making all the cooperating networked nodes work temporarily as a singular, unified entity.

Given such a context, the second class of cooperation defined in this book as supportive protocols should be rather perceived as all the activities preceding the, de facto, collaborative phase. In other words, Network Layer protocols may feed and equip network nodes with all the relevant and cooperation related data still before the collaborative protocol has been triggered. Even though such could be the first impression, this approach does not explicitly pertain to cooperative routing but it rather covers a widespread area of information exchange between or among nodes at the network layer so that their operation and behaviour may be orchestrated well in advance, still before the phase of the collaborative protocol comes into force. An obvious difference is then that this form of cooperation does not require a joint action per se, and, quit the contrary, the act of working with other nodes becomes much more exposed. The class of supportive protocols could be then, equally well, named as a pre-collaborative ones given the fact that they may only settle the ground for the target collaborative protocol. Looking for examples, one could think, for instance, about the mechanism of Fast Re-Routing (FRR), where alternative paths are sought for in advance to potentially quickly re-route the traffic over a back-up connection [17]. Such back-up paths may be, in fact, exploited for the instantiation of the already indicated cooperative relaying, which are, in turn, calling for a consistent collaborative action.

## 4.3   Virtual Multiple Input Multiple Output Channel

Looking bottom-up, down from the physical layer towards the autonomic overlay, one of the key enablers for the instantiation of the aforementioned ACB, as defined in this chapter, is the Virtual Multiple Input Multiple Output (VMIMO) radio channel. In the case of ACB such a channel is assumed to be formed primarily through the cooperation of the participating Relay Nodes (RNs) [17]. More precisely, the concept proposed in this book assumes the extension and elevation of the features of RNs to such an extent that, ultimately, they are replaced with Autonomic Cooperative Nodes (ACNs), as already introduced in Sect. 3.6. In fact, the Virtual Multiple Input Multiple Output approach stems directly from the legacy Multiple Input Multiple Output (MIMO) radio channel usually defined with the aid of the matrix $H_{N \times M}$, which contains the channel coefficients $h_{i,j}$ referring to the wireless links between each pair of the transmitting and receiving antennae $i$ ($1 \leq i \leq N$) and $j$ ($1 \leq j \leq M$), respectively (4.1) [14]:

$$H_{N \times M} = \begin{bmatrix} h_{1,1} & h_{1,2} & \cdots & h_{1,M} \\ h_{2,1} & h_{2,2} & \cdots & h_{2,M} \\ \vdots & \vdots & \ddots & \vdots \\ h_{N,1} & h_{N,2} & \cdots & h_{N,M} \end{bmatrix} \tag{4.1}$$

In the case of the Virtual Multiple Input Multiple Output channel there are two major assumptions, clearly translating into key differences. First of all, the elements of a classic Multi-Element Array (MEA) are assumed to be perceived as the above-mentioned Relay Nodes, once again taking the form of Autonomic Cooperative Nodes in the investigated case. Secondly, but equally importantly, sufficiently tight level of synchronism needs to be provided among Autonomic Cooperative Nodes during the phase of collaborative processing so that proper reception is feasible.

This is exactly where the Virtual Multiple Input Multiple Output channel comes into the global picture of Autonomic Cooperative Behaviour. Generally, should the number of both the transmitting and receiving antennae, expressed as $N$ and $M$, respectively, be equal to 1, it is possible to gain merely about 1 bit/Hz for the increase in the Signal-to-Noise Ratio amounting to 3 dB [5]. However, once the Multi-Element Arrays (MEAs) are employed at both sides of the VMIMO channel, and they are of the same size equal to $N$, the attainable capacity may scale virtually linearly with $N$ [9]. Given this fact, consequently, it becomes feasible to achieve the throughput of almost $N$ bits per Hz [5]. Most conveniently, this phenomenon may be very clearly explained on the basis of the SVD theorem, as described, for example, in [15]. In particular, the channel matrix $H_{N \times M}$ can be rewritten in the following way (4.2):

$$H = UDV^H, \tag{4.2}$$

where $D$ is a non-negative and diagonal matrix of the size $M \times N$, while $U$ and $V$ are unitary matrices of the size $M \times M$ and $N \times N$, respectively, and the upper index $^H$ denotes the operation of Hermitian transposition. Undoubtedly, the strength of the Singular Value Decomposition concept lies in the fact that all those matrices are having non-zero elements on their main diagonals only. Mathematically it means that $UU^H = I_M$ and $VV^H = I_N$, where $I_M$ is an identity matrix of the size $M \times M$, and $I_N$ is an identity matrix of the size $N \times N$ [17]. Similarly, the diagonal entries of $D$ are then equal to the non-negative square roots of the eigenvalues of the matrix $HH^H$, and are denoted by $\lambda$ such that $HH^H y = \lambda y$, where $y$ is an eigenvector of the size $M \times 1$ associated with $\lambda$, fulfilling the condition of $y \neq 0$ [15].

Based on the above, one might already correctly conclude that it is possible to think of an equivalent VMIMO channel comprising solely $k$ uncoupled parallel sub-channels, where $k$ is the rank of the channel matrix $H$, and, thus, is equal to the minimum of both $N$ and $M$, at most. Such a situation is depicted in Fig. 4.2 with the use of generic transmitters and receivers denoted by $TX$ and $RY$, where $1 \leq X \leq N$ and $1 \leq Y \leq M$, or $1 \leq X \leq M$ and $1 \leq Y \leq N$, dependant on whether $N < M$ or $N > M$, respectively. The said generic transmitters and receivers may take either the form of the legacy antennae, or, as in the analysed case, they should be rather

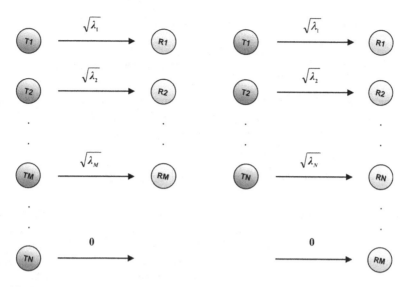

**Fig. 4.2** Equivalent VMIMO channel diagram for both $N < M$ and $N > M$

immediately perceived as Autonomic Cooperative Nodes.[3] Consequently, taking the generic case and assuming theoretically[4] that $N$ is equal to $M$, and, thus, $k$ may be expressed with the value of $N$, the formula defining capacity of such a VMIMO channel could be expressed as (4.3) [15][5]:

$$C = B \log_2 \det \left[ I_N + \frac{P_T}{N\sigma^2} Q \right], \tag{4.3}$$

where $Q$ equals to $HH^H$ for $N > M$ and to $H^H H$ for $N \leq M$, respectively. Keeping in mind that the generic transmitters and receivers are connected exclusively by the aforementioned orthogonal parallel sub-channels, the channel matrix may be expressed as $H = \sqrt{N} I_N$, where $\sqrt{N}$ is a scaling factor pertaining to power normalisation [15]. Following, the VMIMO channel capacity $C$ may be written in the following way, as the existence of a unitary matrix $I_N$ in both the components of the logarithmic function allows for a direct translation into a diagonal matrix having

---

[3]When the generic transmitters and receivers are perceived as Autonomic Cooperative Nodes, certain clarification might be necessary to avoid unintended inconsistency. In particular, the example shown in Fig. 4.2 most directly covers the typical case of Multi-Element Arrays, however, should the said ACNs be homogenous and, thus, equipped with the same number of antennae, then, obviously, $N$ would be always greater than $M$.

[4]For the sake of clearly and directly showing the linear relation between the VMIMO channel capacity and the number of transmitting or receiving antennae or ACNs.

[5]Function det() denotes the determinant.

the relevant expression on its main diagonal: (4.4) [15]:[6]

$$C = B \log_2 \det \left[ I_N + \frac{NP_T}{N\sigma^2} I_N \right] = B \log_2 \det \left[ \mathrm{diag} \left( 1 + \frac{P_T}{\sigma^2} \right) \right]. \tag{4.4}$$

Given the properties of the determinant of such a matrix, making it equivalent to the product of the elements on its main diagonal, as well as applying basic logarithmic operations, the equation may be further rewritten as (4.5) [15]:

$$C = B \log_2 \left( 1 + \frac{P_T}{\sigma^2} \right)^N = NB \log_2 \left( 1 + \frac{P_T}{\sigma^2} \right). \tag{4.5}$$

Based on the above it is directly visible that the capacity of the Virtual Multiple Input Multiple Output channel may, in fact, scale linearly with the number of antennae. The achievable normalised channel capacity is illustrated in Fig. 4.3 assuming an equal number of the transmitting and the receiving antennae, i.e. $N = M$, ranging from 1 up to 8. This indeed proves the claimed attainable and extremely high data

**Fig. 4.3** Capacity of VMIMO channel for the case of $N = M$

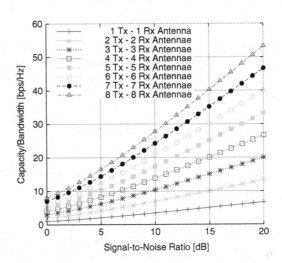

throughputs when the VMIMO systems are concerned. In general, the achievable gain may be exploited in two ways [10]. On the one hand, as it will be chiefly the case in this very book, one may create a highly effective combined transmission and reception diversity scheme for the purposes of increasing the robustness of the system against the impairments induced by the radio channel [16]. On the other hand, instead, one may as well transmit multiple data streams in parallel, and, therefore, increase the quantifiable data throughput [17].

---

[6]The relevant diagonal matrix is denoted by the function diag().

## 4.4 Spatio-Temporal Processing

Most obviously, the instantiation of the Autonomic Cooperative Behaviour for the purposes of exploiting the theoretically achievable capacity gains calls for the application of special spatio-temporal processing techniques. In fact, there are a few such approaches being directly deployable for the needs of pre-processing the transmitted signals in order to make them more robust to the aforementioned impairments of the radio propagation [17]. Among them there is a very neat technique of Spatio-Temporal Block Coding (STBC)[7] offering the, so called, diversity gain but providing zero coding gain [2]. This is why, despite its name, the spatio-temporal block coding is most often perceived as a modulation technique rather than typical coding [17].[8] The base $G_2$ spatio-temporal block code is defined as follows (4.6):

$$G_2 = \begin{bmatrix} x_1 & x_2 \\ -x_2^* & x_1^* \end{bmatrix}. \tag{4.6}$$

This code may be used in a system employing two transmitting and any number of receiving antennae.[9] More specifically, in the first time slot, the $x_1$ and $x_2$ symbols are dispatched by the first and second transmitting antenna, respectively, and then, in the second time slot, the $-x_2^*$ and $x_1^*$ symbols are transmitted alike [2].

Besides, also other spatio-temporal block codes are known, such as, for example, the below presented pairs of $G_3$ and $H_3$ ones for three transmitting antennae (4.7), or the $G_4$ and $H_4$ ones for four transmitting antennae (4.8) [12, 13]. Those higher order codes are especially applicable to Multi-Element Arrays or Virtual Cooperative Sets[10] of greater sizes. One should note, however, that there is a trade-off between the robustness of each of those codes and their rate $R$ being strictly tied with the number of transmitting antennae.[11] In fact, the said code rate is equal to 1 in the case of the $G_2$ code only, while the $H_3$ and $H_4$ codes offer the rate of $\frac{3}{4}$, and the $G_3$

---

[7]This technique has been originally named Space-Time Block Coding, however, the author of this book prefers the name of Spatio-Temporal Block Coding, especially that it allows to maintain the same acronym.

[8]In particular, one of its main advantages for the proposed solution lies with the possibility of shifting the physical complexity related to deploying Multi-Element Arrays (MEAs) on the Destination Node (DN) to creating a Virtual Cooperative Set (VCS) consisting of Autonomic Cooperative Nodes on the retransmitting, or relaying, side.

[9]In Sect. 4.5 it will be shown how this approach may translate into the collaboration of ACNs.

[10]As explained in Sect. 4.5, given the prior introduction of the Autonomic Cooperative Node (ACN) in Sect. 3.6 for the needs of upgrading the legacy Relay Node (RN), similarly the functionality of Virtual Antenna Arrays (VAAs) is extended to Virtual Cooperative Sets (VCSs).

[11]Keeping in mind already the previous indication, even though the term of code rate is used here following the generally assumed nomenclature in the field of Spatio-Temporal Block Coding, it may be misleading as it would rather pertain to a certain type of modulation efficiency, to be more precise.

and $G_4$ ones achieve the rate of $\frac{1}{2}$ [17].

$$
G_3 = \begin{bmatrix} x_1 & x_2 & x_3 \\ -x_2 & x_1 & -x_4 \\ -x_3 & x_4 & x_1 \\ -x_4 & -x_3 & x_2 \\ x_1^* & x_2^* & x_3^* \\ -x_2^* & x_1^* & -x_4^* \\ -x_3^* & x_4^* & x_1^* \\ -x_4^* & -x_3^* & x_2^* \end{bmatrix}, \quad
H_3 = \begin{bmatrix} x_1 & x_2 & \frac{x_3}{\sqrt{2}} \\ -x_2^* & x_1^* & \frac{x_3}{\sqrt{2}} \\ \frac{x_3^*}{\sqrt{2}} & \frac{x_3^*}{\sqrt{2}} & \frac{(-x_1-x_1^*+x_2-x_2^*)}{\sqrt{2}} \\ \frac{x_3^*}{\sqrt{2}} & -\frac{x_3^*}{\sqrt{2}} & \frac{(x_2+x_2^*+x_1-x_1^*)}{\sqrt{2}} \end{bmatrix} \qquad (4.7)
$$

$$
G_4 = \begin{bmatrix} x_1 & x_2 & x_3 & x_4 \\ -x_2 & x_1 & -x_4 & x_3 \\ -x_3 & x_4 & x_1 & -x_2 \\ -x_4 & -x_3 & x_2 & x_1 \\ x_1^* & x_2^* & x_3^* & x_4^* \\ -x_2^* & x_1^* & -x_4^* & x_3^* \\ -x_3^* & x_4^* & x_1^* & -x_2^* \\ -x_4^* & -x_3^* & x_2^* & x_1^* \end{bmatrix}, \quad
H_4 = \begin{bmatrix} x_1 & x_2 & \frac{x_3}{\sqrt{2}} & \frac{x_3}{\sqrt{2}} \\ -x_2^* & x_1^* & \frac{x_3}{\sqrt{2}} & -\frac{x_3}{\sqrt{2}} \\ \frac{x_3^*}{\sqrt{2}} & \frac{x_3^*}{\sqrt{2}} & \frac{(-x_1-x_1^*+x_2-x_2^*)}{\sqrt{2}} & \frac{(-x_2-x_2^*+x_1-x_1^*)}{\sqrt{2}} \\ \frac{x_3^*}{\sqrt{2}} & -\frac{x_3^*}{\sqrt{2}} & \frac{(x_2+x_2^*+x_1-x_1^*)}{\sqrt{2}} & -\frac{(x_1+x_1^*+x_2-x_2^*)}{\sqrt{2}} \end{bmatrix}
$$

$$(4.8)$$

Analysing the general process of reception, a spatio-temporal block decoder could operate solely with the use of a single receiving antenna. However, for the best performance, it would be recommended to use a larger receiving MEA.[12] In particular, the signal received by a receiving antenna $j$ may be then expressed as (4.9):

$$
r_t^j = \sum_{i=1}^{N} h_{i,j} s_t^i + \eta_t^j, \qquad (4.9)
$$

where $h_{i,j}$ denotes the channel coefficient, as previously defined for case of the legacy MIMO channel matrix (4.1), $s_t^i$ represents the symbol dispatched by the transmitting antenna $i$, while the noise samples $\eta_t^j$ are modelled by the complex Gaussian process of a zero mean value and $N_0/2$ variance per dimension [17]. Going further, the key feature of Spatio-Temporal Block Coding, being also the main condition under which the operation of decoding may be successfully performed, is their orthogonality defined as (4.10) [2, 12]:

---

[12]This also holds true for the Distributed Spatio-Temporal Block Coding (DSTBC), to be introduced in Sect. 4.5, where the elements of the MEA are, in fact, replaced with Autonomic Cooperative Nodes (ACNs).

$$G_N G_N^H = \left( \sum_{i=1}^{N} |x_i|^2 \right) I_N, \tag{4.10}$$

where $N$ is equal to the number of transmitting antennae and $I_N$ is an identity matrix of the size $N \times N$. The process of decoding is based on a maximum-likelihood detection aiming to minimise the decision metric given by the formula (4.11) [12]:

$$d = \sum_{t=1}^{L} \sum_{j=1}^{M} \left| r_t^j - \sum_{i=1}^{N} h_{i,j} s_t^i \right|^2. \tag{4.11}$$

## 4.5 Collaborative Transmission Protocols

In the immediately preceding section it was shown that the capacity promised by the Virtual Multiple Input Multiple Output (VMIMO) channel requires a spatio-temporal processing technique to materialise. In particular, while originally the Spatio-Temporal Block Coding (STBC) introduced therein was destined for fixed Multi-Element Arrays (MEAs), its networked version, in the form of Distributed Spatio-Temporal Block Coding (DSTBC) may enable and facilitate collaborative transmission, as defined in Sect. 4.2. Thus, collaborative transmission among Autonomic Cooperative Nodes (ACNs) forming Virtual Cooperative Sets (VCSs) constitutes the next level of Autonomic Cooperative Behaviour (ACB). In particular, the collaborative transmission investigated in this book stems from legacy cooperative relaying also known as cooperation diversity, cooperative diversity, virtual antenna arrays, or coded cooperation [17]. As such, those protocols may be categorised in regard to the forwarding strategy, or the protocol nature [18]. In the first case, one may distinguish the Amplify-and-Forward (AF), Decode-and-Forward (DF), and Decode-and-Reencode (DR) categories. While the Amplify-and-Forward protocols are also referred to as non-regenerative ones, but the Decode-and-Forward and Decode-and-Reencode ones belong to the regenerative category, the Decode-and-Reencode class additionally includes fixed, adaptive, and feedback-based protocols [6].[13]

From the perspective of composing the Autonomic Cooperative Behaviour, it is necessary to orchestrate the operation of Autonomic Cooperative Nodes by putting them in collaboration. This is proposed to be done through the creation of Virtual Cooperative Sets constituted with the use of relevantly modified Multi-Point Relay

---

[13]This categorisation will be further elaborated on in Sect. 5.2 of the following chapter, where the capabilities of the Link Layer, as defined by the Open Systems Interconnection (OSI) Reference Model (RM) will be contrasted with the ones of the Network Layer in order to instantiate cross-layering for the needs of fully integrating the Autonomic Cooperative Behaviour.

(MPR) station selection heuristics,[14] to be described in Sect. 4.6. In particular, as the collaboration between or among ACNs is instantiated through the Distributed Spatio-Temporal Block Coding, the aforementioned VCSs stem from the concept of Virtual Antenna Arrays (VAAs)[15] [4]. In fact, a system employing Distributed Spatio-Temporal Block Coding may be modelled as illustrated in Fig. 4.4, where the process of transmission between the Source Node (SN) and the Destination Node (DN) comprises two phases [8]. During the first phase, the SN broadcasts its signal, which is received by the DN, as well as by the ACNs, potentially expected to engage in collaboration. Afterwards, this signal is processed by those intermediate ACNs and, finally, retransmitted towards the DN within the duration of the second phase [7]. In particular, in this very phase, ACNs should be perceived as being capable of collaboratively encoding the received signals according to a given spatio-temporal block code matrix $X_Y$ by forming the said Virtual Cooperative Set, where $X_Y = \{G_2, G_3, G_4, H_3, H_4\}$.

**Fig. 4.4** Distributed
spatio-temporal block coding

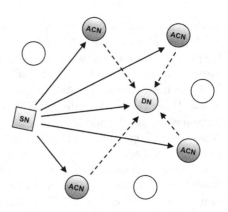

Following, the reference relative data throughput results are presented for Autonomic Cooperative Behaviour based on each of the above codes $X_Y$. To this end an Additive White Gaussian Noise (AWGN) VMIMO channel is exploited and the power emitted by each of the collaboratively relaying ACNs is always normalised so that its total value always amounts to 1. The SINR at the DN is then defined as the total received signal power to the interference and noise power ratio. Each time 50 million bits are transmitted and up to eight receiving antennae are employed. The AWGN channel is used together with the Quadrature Phase Shift Keying (QPSK) modulation. The results showing the achievable performance of the $G_2$, $G_3$ and $H_3$, as well as $G_4$ and $H_4$ are presented in Figs. 4.5, 4.6, and 4.7, respectively. One should

---

[14]The original heuristics is part of the Optimised Link State Routing (OLSR) protocol, while its modified version will become a constituent of the Autonomic Cooperative Networking Protocol (ACNP) to be described in Chap. 5.

[15]In this book the term of Virtual Antenna Arrays is not applied directly as it appears to pertain mostly to the Link Layer, while the proper orchestration of the overall concept presented by the author requires certain conceptual and functional elevation in this respect.

**Fig. 4.5** Reference relative data throughput for G2 based ACB

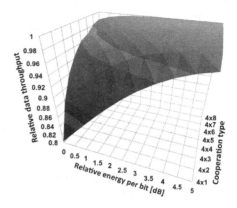

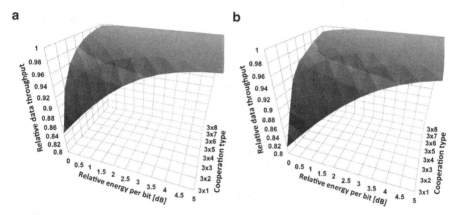

**Fig. 4.6** Reference relative data throughput for G3 and H3 based ACB

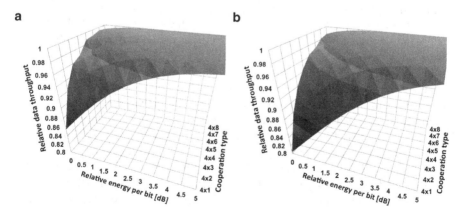

**Fig. 4.7** Reference relative data throughput for G4 and H4 based ACB

note the performance loss visible in the case of the ACB employing the $H_3$ and $H_4$ codes. To account for that it generally suffices to analyse the structure of the pertinent matrices (4.7) and (4.8), where it is conspicuous that in the case of the $H_3$ and $H_4$ codes certain columns are scaled making the process of collaborative transmission suboptimal.

## 4.6   Multi-Point Relay Station Selection Heuristics

Last but not least comes the Multi-Point Relay (MPR) station selection heuristics of the Optimised Link State Routing (OLSR) protocol being the most elevated component of Autonomic Cooperative Behaviour (ACB). In fact, its modified version aims to facilitate the orchestration of collaborative transmission at the Link Layer with the use of additional topology and link state information readily available from the Network Layer. This is possible as the Autonomic Cooperative Nodes selected as MPR stations may, in fact, constitute Virtual Cooperative Sets[16] leading to the instantiation of the desired Autonomic Cooperative Behaviour. While the process of cross-layering and the relevant integration will be explained in the next chapter, here the heuristics itself will be outlined. In general, the MPR station selection heuristics is primarily intended to minimise the OLSR protocol control traffic, most commonly known as the protocol or control overhead [17]. In order to perform the said heuristics, a given source node, let us call it $x$, is obliged to, first of all, collect the necessary information pertaining to its one-hop and two-hop neighbourhoods. For this reason, it exploits the data acquired through the periodical exchange of the so-called Hello messages with its, immediate, one-hop neighbours. In particular, each one-hop neighbour of this source node, let us denote it by $n$, advertises not only its one-hop neighbourhood, but also the status of the corresponding links [3]. Consequently, the node $x$ can identify both its symmetric neighbourhoods and, then, perform the very MPR selection heuristics, as shown in Fig. 4.8. For the needs of outlining the workings of the heuristics, let us also define $N(x)$ as the set of one-hop neighbours and $N^{(2)}(x)$ as the set two-hop neighbours of node $x$.

Going further, $MPR(x)$ denotes a set of Multi-Point Relays of the node $x$, where an MPR is a node which was selected by its one-hop neighbour $x$ to retransmit all the broadcast messages that it receives from this node, provided that a message to be retransmitted is not a duplicate and its Time To Live (TTL) field carries value greater than one [3]. The MPR selection heuristics is performed with the use of both the sets of one-hop and two-hop neighbours [17]. First, the node $x$ includes in its $MPR(x)$ set all those of its symmetric one-hop neighbours $n$ which are the only ones to provide reachability to a node $n^2$, located in the strict symmetric two-hop neighbourhood, and additionally are always willing to carry and forward traffic [11].

---

[16]Stemming from Virtual Antenna Arrays (VAAs) [17].

**Fig. 4.8** Multi-point relay
station selection heuristics

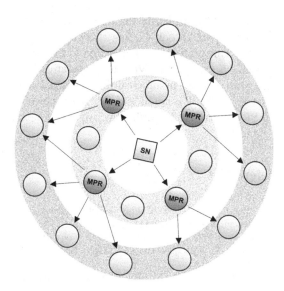

Next, while there still exist any uncovered nodes in $N^2(x)$ the heuristics keeps on
selecting that node $n$ from the set $N(x)$ which has not been inserted into the $MPR(x)$
set thus far, and is characterised by the highest willingness to carry and forward
traffic. In the case of multiple choices, the one is chosen which provides the highest
reachability $R(n)$, i.e. through which the highest number of still uncovered nodes
in the set $N^2(x)$ may be reached. Otherwise, if it is impossible to select one node
only, the node with the highest degree is chosen, where the degree $D(n)$ of a one-
hop neighbour $n$ denotes the number of its symmetric neighbours, excluding all the
members of $N(x)$ and the node $x$ performing the computation [3]. Once the MPR
selection procedure is completed, Topology Control messages can be disseminated
solely via this limited set of identified MPR nodes, which constructively contributes
to a significant reduction of the control overhead [11].

## 4.7 Conclusion

In this chapter, the concept of Autonomic Cooperative Behaviour was introduced
at the lowest level of the analysed three-tier Autonomic Cooperative System
Architectural Model, under which the ACB is composed with the aid of creating
Virtual Cooperative Sets (VCSs) being orchestrated by the Autonomic Cooperative
Networking Protocol. In fact, the ACB was shown not only to be multi-faceted but
also hardly definable. To account for its role and meaning, first of all the notion of
cooperation was introduced as a distinguishing element between the defined collaborative and supportive protocols. Following, the Virtual Multiple Input Multiple
Output (VMIMO) channel was outlined as the main enabler for an efficient instan-

tiation of ACB, primarily through a properly tailored application of Distributed Spatio-Temporal Block Coding (DSTBC) among Autonomic Cooperative Nodes (ACNs). This phase was emphasised to expose the above-mentioned composition of ACB on the basis of Virtual Cooperative Sets. The process of VCSs creation itself was, in turn, assumed to be integrated into and orchestrated by the Multi-Point Relay (MPR) station selection heuristics of the Optimised Link State Routing (OLSR) protocol to be further investigated in next chapter.

# References

1. Collins Cobuild (1997). *Collins Cobuild english dictionary*. New York: HarperCollins.
2. Alamouti, S. (1998). A simple transmit diversity technique for wireless communications. *IEEE Journal on Selected Areas in Communications, 16*(8), 1451–1458.
3. Clausen, T., & Jacquet, P. (2003). Optimised link state routing protocol (OLSR). *RFC 3626, IETF*.
4. Dohler, M., & Li, Y. (2010). *Cooperative communications - hardware, channel & PHY*. New York: Wiley.
5. Foschini, G. J., & Gans, M. J. (1998). On limits of wireless communications in fading environment when using multiple antennas. *Wireless Personal Communications, 6*, 311–335.
6. Herhold, P., Zimmermann, E., & Fettweis, G. (2005). Cooperative multi-hop transmission in wireless networks. *Computer Networks Journal, 49*(3), 299–324.
7. Laneman, J. N., Tse, D. N. C., & Wornell, G. W. (2004). Cooperative diversity in wireless networks: Efficient protocols and outage behavior. *IEEE Transactions on Information Theory, 50*(12), 3062–3080.
8. Laneman, J. N., & Wornell, G. W. (2003). Distributed space-time-coded protocols for exploiting cooperative diversity in wireless networks. *IEEE Transactions on Information Theory, 49*(10), 2415–2425.
9. Lozano, A., Farrokhi, F. R., & Valenzuela, R. A. (2001). Lifting the limits on high-speed wireless data access using antenna arrays. *IEEE Communications Magazine, 39*(9), 156–162.
10. Molisch, A. F., & Win, M. Z. (2004). MIMO Systems with antenna selection. *IEEE Microwave Magazine, 5*(4), 46–56.
11. Qayyum, A., Viennot, L., & Laouiti, A. (2002). Multipoint relaying for flooding broadcast messages in mobile wireless networks. In: *35th Annual Hawaii International Conference on System Sciences, HICSS*.
12. Tarokh, V., Jafarkhani, H., & Calderbank, A. R. (1999). Space-time block codes from orthogonal designs. *IEEE Transactions on Information Theory, 45*(5), 1456–1467.
13. Tarokh, V., Jafarkhani, H., & Calderbank, A. R. (1999). Space-time block coding for wireless communications: Performance results. *IEEE Journal on Selected Areas in Communications, 17*(3), 451–460.
14. Telatar, I. E. (1999). Capacity of multi-antenna Gaussian channels. *European Transactions on Telecommunications, 10*(6), 585–595.
15. Vucetic, B., & Yuan, J. (2003). *Space-time coding*. New York: Wiley.
16. Wódczak, M. (2005). On the Adaptive approach to antenna selection and space-time coding in context of the relay based mobile Ad-hoc networks. In: *XI National Symposium of Radio Science URSI* (pp. 138–142), Poznań, Poland.
17. Wódczak, M. (2012). *Autonomic cooperative networking*. New York: Springer.
18. Zimmermann, E., Herhold, P., & Fettweis, G. (2005). On the performance of cooperative relaying in wireless networks. *European Transactions on Telecommunications, 16*(1), 5–16.

# Chapter 5
# Autonomic Cooperative Networking Protocol

## 5.1 Introduction

Following the introduction of the notion of Autonomic Cooperative Behaviour
(ACB) in the previous chapter, the bottom-up description of the proposed
Autonomic Cooperative System Architectural Model (ACSAM) is continued
with the outlining of the workings of the Autonomic Cooperative Networking
Protocol (ACNP). In fact, the ACNP protocol is a cross-layer solution which is
may be perceived as a bit biased towards the Network Layer of the Open Systems
Interconnection (OSI) Reference Model (RM), however, on the other hand, it is
profoundly rooted in the Distributed Spatio-Temporal Block Coding (DSTBC)
of the Link Layer, in fact, going down even to the Physical Layer when the
orchestration of the underlying Virtual Multiple Input Multiple Output (VMIMO)
is concerned. In particular, once the motivation for the said cross-layering has
been explained, the relevant context of the Optimised Link State Routing (OLSR)
protocol is introduced to form the basis for its extension, the ACNP. Following,
the integration of the tightly related ACB is described with a special emphasis
on its composition with the aid of the Multi-Point Relay (MPR) station selection
heuristics. This part is complemented with the proposed messaging structure along
with the detailing of the functioning of ACNP itself in terms of assigning Autonomic
Cooperative Nodes (ACNs) to Virtual Cooperative Sets (VCSs). Eventually, the
analysis of the expected overhead induced by the OLSR-ACNP tandem is carried
out to establish the region of safe and efficient operation.

## 5.2 Motivation for Cross-Layering

Following the context settled in Sect. 4.5, where various collaborative protocols of
the Link Layer were introduced, as well as keeping in mind the need for orchestration of the Autonomic Cooperative Nodes (ACNs) forming Virtual Cooperative

M. Wódczak, *Autonomic Computing Enabled Cooperative Networked Design*,
SpringerBriefs in Computer Science, DOI 10.1007/978-1-4939-0764-9_5,
© The Author(s) 2014

Sets (VCSs) with the aid of certain Network Layer routines of the sort of the Multi-Point Relay (MPR) station selection heuristics, as advocated for in Sect. 4.6, it becomes of prime importance to scrutinise the need for a cross-layered approach [12]. Clearly, it is so, as the Optimised Link State Routing (OLSR) protocol, being the basis for Autonomic Cooperative Networking Protocol (ACNP), already offers certain options for the integration of lower layer mechanisms. In particular, it appears that such a necessity is conditioned most naturally and there is not really much leeway in this respect. In other words, even though the three categories of collaborative protocols functioning at the Link Layer, i.e. the Amplify-and-Forward (AF), Decode-and-Forward (DF), and Decode-and-Reencode (DR) protocols, are already sufficiently complicated to serve certain basic collaboration types, they are not able to accommodate the orchestration of collaborative transmission or transmissions on a broader scale. Obviously, it would be possible to implement all the necessary and relevant extensions but then the operation of the Link Layer could become somewhat overloaded and unbalanced, if not entirely warped. For this reason, in order to keep the distinct layers of the Open Systems Interconnection (OSI) Reference Model (RM) hermetic and, at the same time, provide the overall required functionality, it is a far better idea to combine the operation of the two adjacent layers through the mechanism of cross-layering.

In fact, already analysing the general naming structure pertaining to both the Link Layer and the Network Layer, one might come to a conclusion that, at least at first sight, in each case there is a notion of a protocol. However, looking deeper there appears a huge discrepancy to be arising between what the word "protocol" may actually mean in the context of those layers. In articular, as indicated above, when the issue is perceived from the angle of the Link Layer, the connotation of the word "protocol" is more resembling a "scheme" meaning a not very complicated sequence of operations or interactions, designed for a specific purpose. Even though there may be, and definitely is, certain dose of dynamism, the overall approach is positioned far away from the ad hoc operation of the proactive Network Layer protocol, such as the Optimised Link State Routing (OLSR) one. In this case, the word "protocol" denotes much more, as its semantic field rather covers all the pertinent control information exchange, messaging formats, repositories, and, only then, certain very dynamically changeable schemes related to data routing. The operation of such a protocol covers much more that just overseeing a couple or several nodes. It is intended to orchestrate the functioning of the whole domain or even the entire network. This is why, the Autonomic Cooperative Networking Protocol (ACNP) should be seen more as a combination of the two layers, seeking for the synergy between them. The synergy is expected to manifest itself through the ability of ACNP to use and combine, in an autonomic manner, certain specific Network Layer mechanisms, such as the Multi-Point Relay (MPR) station selection heuristics to orchestrate the collaborating Autonomic Cooperative Nodes (ACNs) at the Link Layer.

Interestingly, the aforementioned categories of collaborative protocols may be analysed from both the forwarding strategy and protocol nature viewpoints [15]. Thanks to their resemblance of a scheme, as indicated above, their operation, understood as the said forwarding strategy, may be explained directly with the use of the nomenclature of the field of autonomics. The most baseline solution among those protocols, known as Amplify-and-Forward, operates on the basis of the assumption that before retransmission may take place, the legacy Relay Node (RN), in the case of the proposed solution elevated functionally to Autonomic Cooperative Node, would need to acts as an analogue repeater [10]. Unfortunately, even though the received signal would become amplified, the noise would get enhanced in the same manner and, thus, this approach is of no interest for the Autonomic Cooperative Networking Protocol. Two other approaches, known as Decode-and-Forward and Decode-and-Reencode seem to fit much better into the workings of ACNP, however. While the former of them would assume the ACN to attempts to fully decode, regenerate and reencode the received signal before a retransmission may take place, the latter would not only perform the steps of fully decoding and regenerating the received signal but it would additionally construct a new code word, different from the source one, in order to enable advanced channel coding. Even though it is claimed that in both the cases there would potentially occur the propagation of decoding errors, leading to wrong decisions at the destination [18], it appears that the additional intelligence introduced by Autonomic Cooperative Nodes should definitely discard such a possibility.

Taking into account the protocol nature, in turn, there are, similarly, the following three options available: fixed, adaptive, or feedback-based schemes [18]. According to the fixed approach, an ACN would always, possibly also after having performed some relevant processing, forward the received signal. Unfortunately, as such a behaviour of a networked system might not be advisable in every situation, thankfully, an additional dose of automation, so necessary for the proper operation of Autonomic Cooperative Networking Protocol, is introduced by the adaptive and feedback-based schemes. In particular, while the former of them would assume an ACN to autonomically decide whether to forward the received signal or not, the latter would require that an ACN assist in the transmission only when it receives an explicit request from the Destination Node (DN) [15]. As it is clearly visible, the adaptive and feedback-based schemes might efficiently integrate into the overall concept of Decision Elements (DEs), as advocated for by the Generic Autonomic Network Architecture (GANA), introduced previously in Sect. 3.3 [16]. More specifically, the ability of taking an automatic decision in the adaptive approach would translate directly into the orchestration performed by a DE steering the said scheme as a Managed Entity (ME) within an Autonomic Control Loop (ACL) running on the protocol level of the GANA abstraction. Similarly, the feedback-based scheme would assume additional indication coming, most usually, given the hierarchical approach, from a higher level DE, or, in certain but rather rare cases, also possibly from a peer DE.

## 5.3  Optimised Link State Routing

As it was primarily designed for MANETs, the Optimised Link State Routing protocol appears a perfect fit for the developed concept [5]. One of its key advantages is the fact that it is a working and deployable protocol, currently being upgraded to the second version [4]. In general, the dynamism inherent in ad hoc environments may manifest itself in highly frequent changes in network topology [2]. This may create a requirement that a protocol be tailored accordingly to maintain a reasonably moderate control overhead while being able to provide accurate routing information [13]. Depending on the level of the said dynamism, one might distinguish among three classes of routing protocols [1]. First of all, there is a proactive approach where each network node performs topology recognition on a regular basis in order to keep the routing tables always up-to-date. Unfortunately, unless optimised, such an approach might turn out costly in terms of the said control overhead.[1] Secondly, a reactive approach exists in the case of which the operation of topology recognition is performed solely when the routing table needs to be updated. Consequently, the control overhead may be reduced, but, on the other hand, the delay related to selecting a proper route is bound to increase. Last but not least there is a hybrid approach which combines the advantages of both the aforementioned classes by applying either of them in accordance with the activity of mobile networked nodes in specific regions. As long as the topology changes remain insignificant, the reactive attitude may be more appropriate, otherwise, when the dynamism raises, the proactive one is used.

In order to provide a sufficient context for the introduction of the workings of Autonomic Cooperative Networking Protocol (ACNP), the format of the OLSR Hello Message will be described below (Fig. 5.1), as it comprises certain extendable parameters of high importance from the perspective of not only enabling the ACNP, but instantiating the very ACB, in particular. The message starts with a split

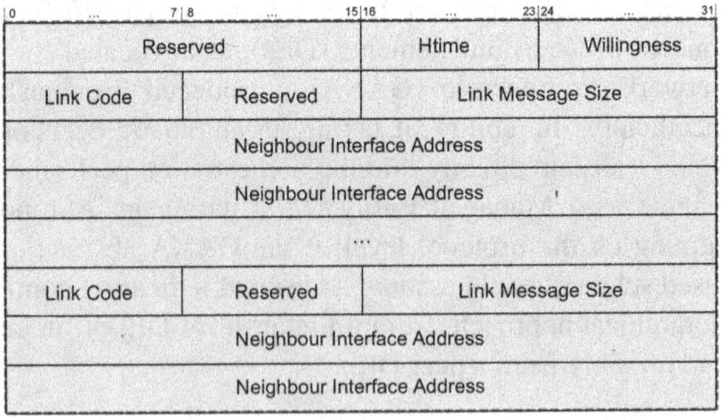

**Fig. 5.1**  Hello message

---

[1] Also known as protocol overhead or protocol control overhead.

Reserved field of 24 bits in total, currently reserved and required to contain a fixed sequence of 0000000000000000.[2] Next is the Htime (Holding time) field of 8 bits specifying the emission interval between dispatching Hello Messages from a given interface. This interval is represented in the form of the mantissa $a$, i.e. the four Most Significant Bits (MSBs), along with the exponent $b$, i.e. the four Least Significant Bits (LSBs), and it is calculated according to the following formula (5.1)[3]:

$$H_t = C\left(1 + \frac{a}{16}\right)2^b, \quad C = \frac{1}{16} = 0.0625s. \tag{5.1}$$

Even though the predefined emission interval of Hello Messages is equal to 2 s, it can, in fact, range from 62.6 ms up to almost 2.28 h. A very important, from the perspective of autonomics, Willingness field of 8 bits follows specifying whether a given node would be willing to carry and forward traffic to other nodes or not. There are the following levels of willingness available: WILL_NEVER (0), WILL_LOW (1), WILL_DEFAULT (3), WILL_HIGH (6), and WILL_ALWAYS (7).[4] Next crucial field is the Link Code of 8 bits specifying the type of the link between an interface of a given node and the listed interfaces of its neighbours, along with indicating the neighbour type, as depicted in Fig. 5.2. Following there is the Link Message Size filed of 16 bits containing the size of the Link Message expressed in bytes, counting from the beginning of a given Link Code, until the beginning of the next Link Code field, or, should there be no more link types, until the end of the message. Eventually, there appears the Neighbour Interface Address of 16 bits specifying the address of an interface of a given neighbour node.

As outlined in previous chapter, the Autonomic Cooperative Behaviour (ACB) is multi-faceted and spans over different layers of the Open Systems Interconnection (OSI) Reference Model (RM). It is then of prime importance to establish the manner in which ACB is integrated into the Autonomic Cooperative Networking Protocol, proposed to be, in fact, a cross-layer protocol itself. In other words, this section outlines the rationale behind the fusion of Virtual Cooperative Set (VCS) enabled collaborative transmission protocol, based on the concept of Autonomic Cooperative Nodes (ACNs), with the messaging format and Multi-Point Relay (MPR) station selection heuristics of the Optimised Link State Routing (OLSR) protocol. The fusion is then taking place on two abstract levels, let us call them the structural and the functional ones. The former pertains to the necessary modifications and extensions to the said messaging format and the related repositories, while the latter encompasses the required upgrading of the above-mentioned MPR station selection

---

[2]While 16 and 8 zeros would be expected, respectively, the specification provides solely a zeroed sequence of the length of 13 [5].

[3]As defined in the specification, $C$ is a constant scaling factor [5].

[4]One should note, however, that should the willingness be set to 0, a given node must never be selected as an MPR station, whereas, on the contrary, in the case of willingness equal to 7, such a node must always be selected an MPR station.

heuristics together with the exposition and actual exploitation of the Autonomic Cooperative Behaviour enabling feature of the willingness to carry and forward traffic.

## 5.4   Integration of Autonomic Cooperative Behaviour

Following the description of the format of the Hello Message given in the previous section, the structure of the Link Code (8 bits), defining the type of the link between a given interface and the neighbour interfaces, along with indicating the neighbour type, is depicted in Fig. 5.2. Currently, there are 16 different combinations plausible, however, as future extensions have been also predicted in the specification, this possibility will be used for the ACB integration-related purposes. In fact, the Link

**Fig. 5.2** *Link code* format

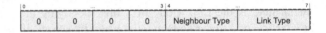

Code is structured in such a way that each of the Neighbour Type and Link Type fields is assigned two bits [15]. Starting from the Link Type, one should note that, in general, a symmetric link is defined as a verified bi-directional link between two OLSR interfaces, whereas an asymmetric link is defined as link between two OLSR interfaces but verified in one direction only [5]. In particular, there are four values distinguished: UNSPEC_LINK (0) indicating that no information about a given link is specified, ASYM_LINK (1) denoting a given link as asymmetric in the sense that it may only be heard, SYM_LINK (2) classifying a given link as symmetric, and LOST_LINK (3) disqualifying a given link for being not available. Having different link types introduced it becomes much more straightforward to outline the Neighbour Type field. Originally, the OLSR protocol distinguishes among three values, and this fact will be used for the needs of the Autonomic Cooperative Networking Protocol. Yet, according to the specification, there are the following values: NOT_NEIGH (0) denoting a given node as no longer considered as or having not yet become a symmetric neighbour of the source node, SYM_NEIGH (1) indicating that there exists at least one symmetric link between the source node and each of its listed neighbours, and MPR_NEIGH (2) pointing out that there exists at least one symmetric link between the source node and each of its listed neighbours in addition selected as MPRs.

Moreover, based on the classification of links and neighbours, the specification identifies the following neighbourhood types [5]. First of all, a symmetric one-hop neighbourhood of a given source node is most naturally defined as a set of nodes which have at least one symmetric link to this source node. Following, a symmetric two-hop neighbourhood of a given source node is understood as a set of nodes, excluding this source node itself, which have a symmetric link to the symmetric one-hop neighbourhood of this source node. Finally, a symmetric strict two-hop neighbourhood of a given source node denotes a set of nodes, excluding both the source node itself and its neighbours, the members of which have a symmetric link to a symmetric one-hop neighbour of this source node and are characterised by the willingness different from WILL_NEVER. The notion of all the above parameters has been, in fact, already used a bit indirectly, when the Multi-Point Relay station selection heuristics was introduced in the previous chapter in the context of Fig. 4.8. In fact, looking at the positioning of the MPRs in the said Fig. 4.8 from the Network Layer perspective and comparing it with Fig. 4.4 pertinent to the Link Layer it becomes more conspicuous in what way the cross-layering may facilitate the related composition and orchestration of Autonomic Cooperative Behaviour by means of the instantiation of Virtual Cooperative Sets between or among Autonomic Cooperative Nodes.

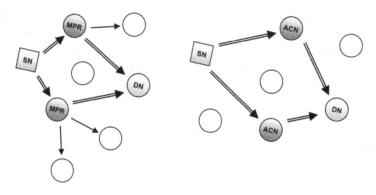

**Fig. 5.3** Integration between MPRs and ACNs

The said integration between MPRs and ACNs is illustrated in Fig. 5.3. In fact, the presented approach stems directly from and builds on top of the idea of Routing information Enhanced Algorithm for Cooperative Transmission (REACT) based on the classic MPR station selection heuristics, and intended to facilitate the process of the organisation of Virtual Antenna Array (VAA)[5] aided cooperative transmission [11]. Even though the concept of VAAs is elevated to Virtual Cooperative Sets (VCSs) and the notion of the legacy Relay Nodes (RNs) is replaced with Autonomic Cooperative Nodes (ACNs), the main idea consists in executing the MPR station selection heuristics iteratively to identify the ACNs which can act together as VCSs and, thus, expose Autonomic Cooperative Behaviour. In fact, being a Network Layer protocol, each OLSR node may acquire the knowledge describing their one-hop and two-hop neighbourhoods [15]. What is more, as it is possible to identify these one-hop neighbours in $N(x)$ which can provide connectivity to some two-hop neighbours in $N^{(2)}(x)$, only those nodes are identified as MPRs help minimise the protocol

---

[5]For additional details on this technology the reader is referred directly to [6].

control overhead. Interestingly, the very same ACNs may enter into collaborative transmission and, this way, display Autonomic Cooperative Behaviour.

As already indicated, the proposed Autonomic Cooperative Networking Protocol (ACNP) derives from the Distributed Spatio-Temporal Block Coding (DSTBC) based Link Layer collaborative transmission protocol [8]. At the same time it directly integrates into and extends the Multi-Point Relay (MPR) station selection heuristics of the Network Layer Optimised Link State Routing (OLSR) protocol. Given the fact that the functionality of the Link Layer, as defined by the Open Systems Interconnection (OSI) Reference Model (RM), can be at most of use for organising collaboration within the local scope, this layer becomes rather integrated than substantially modified [15]. In fact, those are the Network Layer routines and schemes to provide all the logic necessary for the incorporation of the Virtual Multiple Input Multiple Output (VMIMO)[6] based and DSTBC orchestrated collaborative transmission [9]. Such collaboration is instantiated by means of the composition of Autonomic Cooperative Behaviour through allocating Autonomic Cooperative Nodes to their respective Virtual Cooperative Sets (VCSs) with the aid of MPR station selection heuristics. Consequently, the proposed protocol is somewhere in between the two OSI layers, and it becomes a fully-fledged solution when used with the Optimised Link State Routing protocol. The proper operation of Autonomic Cooperative Networking Protocol is possible after certain modifications to OLSR itself are materialised on the basis of the introductory and context-setting information provided in two previous sections.

## 5.5  Message Structure and Protocol Functioning

The above-mentioned modifications are proposed with special attention being paid to making any changes compliant with the OLSR specification [5]. In fact, on the one hand, the ACNP is built around and on top of the Routing information Enhanced Algorithm for Cooperative

Transmission (REACT) [7]. On the other hand, however, it is designed with the intention of making it upgraded to and complaint with the autonomic system architecture as advocated for by the Generic Autonomic Network Architecture (GANA) [17]. At some points, however, the modifications cannot be completely transparent and in such cases the OLSR protocol is patched appropriately in order to make the OLSR-ACNP tandem work properly. Thankfully, the assumption of full backward compatibility is fully met in the case of the first of them, related to the introduction of a new Neighbour Type, where an unallocated Neighbour Type value is exploited [15]. Such a modification is necessary for the purposes of configuring the Virtual Cooperative Sets, and, more specifically, once the VCS pre-

---

[6]This way, the proposed Autonomic Cooperative Networking Protocol additionally goes beyond the Link Layer, down to the Physical Layer.

**Table 5.1**  New ACB neighbour type

| Neighbour type | Value | Description |
|---|---|---|
| ACB_NEIGH | 3 | Indicates that there exists at least one symmetric link between the Source Node and each of its listed neighbours able to act as Autonomic Cooperative Nodes and, therefore, capable of exposing Autonomic Cooperative Behaviour |

selection phase has been completed, each of the chosen ACNs must be informed about having been assigned to a specific $VCS(x, n^{(2)})$ set. In this way, the ACNs are able to conclude in what manner they are supposed to collaboratively process the signals received from the SN. To this end, the list of Neighbour Types, as originally specified by the OLSR protocol and summarised in Sect. 5.4, is extended by adding a new ACB_NEIGH type. The introduction of such a new Neighbour Type, as described in Table 5.1, means that Hello Messages may immediately convey Link Messages of a new class, in fact, determined by the ACB_NEIGH value.

However, as the Link Type information is still fairly rough and imprecise, for accuracy of the Autonomic Cooperative Networking Protocol, additionally, the four Most Significant Bits (MSBs) of the Link Code field are proposed to be utilised together with the eight additional bits of the Reserved field [15]. Such an allocation

**Fig. 5.4**  Extended link code

makes it twelve bits in total available for a new, technically split but functionally consistent, Power Level field, as outlined in Fig. 5.4. Consequently, a new 16 bit Extended Link Code, comprising both the classic Link Code and Reserved fields, is introduced, which results in a Modified Hello Message presented in Fig. 5.5. This way, a given Source Node is not only able to find out, whether its specific one-

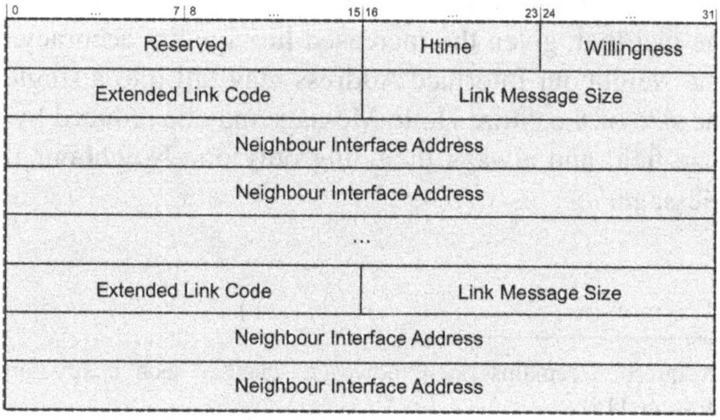

**Fig. 5.5**  Modified hello message

hop neighbour can hear the signal transmitted by this SN, but it may also learn what is the precise power level of this signal. Moreover, as Hello Message sent by such a one-hop neighbour usually contains similar information pertaining also to its own one-hop neighbours, which, in turn, may turn out to be the two-hop neighbours of the Source Node itself, the very SN may have a far more concrete overview of the link parameters in its entire one-hop and two-hop neighbourhoods, especially when the radio channel reciprocity could be assumed. However, this very modification to the Hello Message format is not completely transparent to the workings of the Optimised Link State Routing protocol. Namely, unlike it was the case for the first modification, where it was sufficient to make the protocol aware of the new ACB_NEIGH type, this extension seems to require more attention.

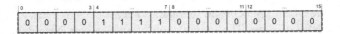

**Fig. 5.6** Extended link code mask

The problem lies with the fact that the Reserved field is utilised which, according to the specification, should remain unchanged [15]. Moreover, the aforementioned four MSBs are exploited which are meant for future extensions, however, not necessarily of the sort of the proposed modification. Therefore, in order to overcome this issue, should a Hello Message be processed for the purposes of performing the classic protocol operations, the new Extended Link Code field would have to be masked with the Extended Link Code Mask, as depicted in Fig. 5.6. In other words, solely for backward compliance reasons, any implementation of the proposed Autonomic Cooperative Networking Protocol would have to utilise the defined Extended Link Code Mask to effect the logical AND operation over all the Extended Link Codes of a given Modified Hello Message. The only exception to this rule would be the case of the Power Level field being required to be accessed for the needs acquiring a more detailed link state information. Even though such an approach may seem to be the safest way for guaranteeing compatibility, one could also consider the introduction of a new Generalised Hello Message format, as outlined in Fig. 5.7 [15]. Its format differs from the legacy Hello Message even further, as it lacks the Link Message Size field at all. This solution is dictated by the fact that, given the increased link quality accuracy, in most of the cases solely one Neighbour Interface Address may fall into a single Link Message. Therefore, the size of the entire Hello Message may be reduced by skipping the Link Message Size field and always including only one Neighbour Interface Address in a Link Message.[7]

---

[7]A question remains open, however, whether such a structure could be still called a Link Message [15].

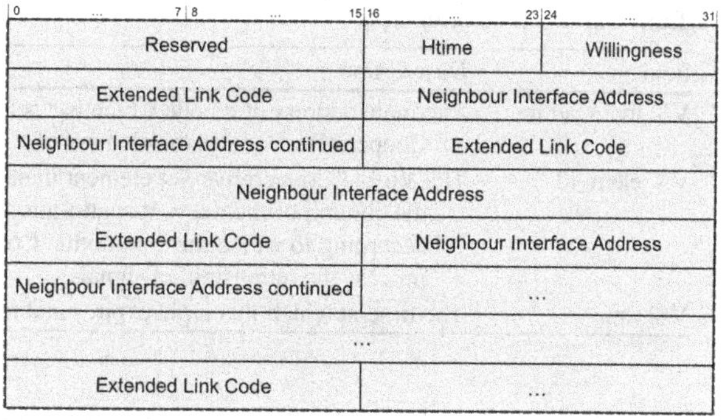

**Fig. 5.7** Generalised hello
message

| 0 ... 7 | 8 ... 15 | 16 ... 23 | 24 ... 31 |
|---|---|---|---|
| Reserved | | Htime | Willingness |
| Extended Link Code | | Neighbour Interface Address | |
| Neighbour Interface Address continued | | Extended Link Code | |
| Neighbour Interface Address | | | |
| Extended Link Code | | Neighbour Interface Address | |
| Neighbour Interface Address continued | | ... | |
| | ... | | |
| Extended Link Code | | ... | |

Going back to the new ACB_NEIGH neighbour type, the idea for the creation of Virtual Cooperative Sets and the instantiation of Distributed Spatio-Temporal Block Coding could be to exploit the order in which the Neighbour Interface Addresses of ACB_NEIGH type are located on the list of the Neighbour Interface Addresses. Such information could be used for the purposes of notifying the pertinent Autonomic Cooperative Nodes about the way they are supposed to collaborate during the retransmission phase. In other words, the position on the list would determine the column of the relevant spatio-temporal block code matrix, according to which each of the ACNs, belonging to a given $VCS(x, n^{(2)})$, should collaboratively process the retransmitted signal. The reciprocal of the number of addresses on such a list would specify the power scaling factor. However, given the introduction of the Extended Link Code, one should note that the power may not be scaled in this way anymore. As already mentioned, since the Modified Hello Messages carry a more detailed link state information, it is rather unlikely that two Neighbour Interface Addresses would fall into one Link Message. Therefore, it should be rather guaranteed that the order of such single element Link Messages would correspond to the columns of the relevant spatio-temporal block code matrix [3]. Yet, even though unlikely, it might be the case that two or more Neighbour Interface Addresses of the ACB_NEIGH type would still fall into the same Link Message, after all.

For this reason, the optimum and safe approach would be to include solely one Neighbour Interface Addresses of an ACB_NEIGH type in a Link Message, and, additionally, to place all such messages in a given Hello Message in the first order to avoid fragmentation.[8] Last but not least, having processed a Modified Hello Message, each Autonomic Cooperative Node of the ACB_NEIGH type needs to store the relevant data [15]. To this end, an additional ACB Selector Set is proposed to be maintained in the Neighbour Information Base.[9] Such a new ACB Selector Set would be then formed by the so-called ACB-Selector Tuples of the

---

[8]This additionally implies that the Generalised Hello Message could be more applicable, however, it would come at the cost of losing the backward compatibility with the original OLSR protocol.

[9]For further information on the repositories of the OLSR protocol the reader is referred directly to the specification [5].

**Table 5.2** ACB-selector tuple

| Item | Description |
|---|---|
| VS_main_addr | The main address of a node which has selected this Autonomic Cooperative Node as the element of a Virtual Cooperative Set |
| VS_elem_id | The Virtual Cooperative Set element identification number specifying the column of the relevant spatio-temporal block code matrix, according to which the Autonomic Cooperative Node should process the retransmitted signals |
| VS_time | The time at which this tuple expires and must be removed |

format presented in Table 5.2. Consequently, each Autonomic Cooperative Node could easily determine if it is to express Autonomic Cooperative Behaviour through collaboration through a simple comparison of its address with the VS_main_addr. Should it be the case, the ACN would use the relevant column of the spatio-temporal block code matrix, as specified by VS_elem_id.

## 5.6  Control Overhead

As already indicated, unless applied correctly, the introduction of a more precise link state information could potentially have a reverse effect on the effectiveness of the proposed Autonomic Cooperative Networking Protocol, because the higher the accuracy, the smaller the number of Autonomic Cooperative Nodes to be assigned to a single Link Message. The reason for such an increase is chiefly the Extended Link Code. Most typically, the OLSR protocol distinguishes among four different Link Types and three different Neighbour Types [14]. This gives twelve combinations in total meaning that all the Neighbour Interface Addresses may be, at most, qualified to twelve Link Messages. For the proposed solution it suffices, when only some of the said Link Messages are separated into smaller sets through the inclusion of extra information about the power level. In particular, due to the type of the required data, it is sufficient to focus on the SYM_LINK, as well as on the SYM_NEIGH and MPR_NEIGH [15]. This limits the number of the theoretically possible sixteen combinations, resulting from the introduction of the ACB_NEIGH, to merely two. The main factor influencing the protocol control overhead is then the size of the Power Level field [14]. As that field is 12 bits long, there are 4,096 values plausible which multiplied by the aforementioned two combinations give 8,192 possibilities. Taking into account the fact that there are only singular interfaces characterised by a given power level, in the worst case, one would end up with 8,192 Link Messages, each accompanied by a header of the length of 32 bits. This is, of course, the worst possibility and Fig. 5.8 presents the expected overhead for different number of bits used. One can see that for 6 bits the control overhead is almost diminishable.

**Fig. 5.8** Overhead of
original, modified, and
generalised hello message

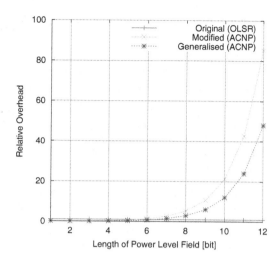

## 5.7   Conclusion

In this chapter the workings of the Autonomic Cooperative Networking Protocol
(ACNP), as an extension to the Optimised Link State Routing (OLSR) protocol,
were outlined. In fact, the ACNP protocol is a cross-layer solution going beyond
the Network Layer of the Open Systems Interconnection (OSI) Reference Model
(RM), as it is profoundly based on the Distributed Spatio-Temporal Block Coding
(DSTBC) of the Link Layer and, in fact, it even reaches the Physical Layer for
the orchestration of the Virtual Multiple Input Multiple Output (VMIMO) enabled
collaborative transmission. In particular, the motivation for the said cross-layering
was explained and the relevant context of the Optimised Link State Routing (OLSR)
protocol was introduced. Following, the integration of the ACB was described
and a special emphasis was laid on its composition with the aid of the Multi-
Point Relay (MPR) station selection heuristics. Moreover, the proposed messaging
structure was detailed together with the functioning of ACNP itself in terms
of assigning Autonomic Cooperative Nodes (ACNs) to Virtual Cooperative Sets
(VCSs). Eventually, the analysis of the expected overhead induced by the ACNP
was carried out to identify the region of safe and efficient operation.

## References

1. Abolhasan, M., Wysocki, T., & Lipman, J. (2005). Performance investigation on three classes
   of MANET routing protocols. In: *Asia-Pacific Conference on Communications* (pp. 774–778).
2. Adjih, C., Baccelli, E., & Jacquet, P. (2003). Link state routing in wireless ad-hoc networks.
   *IEEE Military Communications Conference, MILCOM* (pp. 13–16).
3. Alamouti, S. (1998). A simple transmit diversity technique for wireless communications. *IEEE
   Journal on Selected Areas in Communications, 16*(8), 1451–1458.

4. Clausen, T., Dearlove, C., Jacquet, P., & Herberg, U. (2013). The optimized link state routing protocol version 2. *IETF mobile Ad hoc networking (MANET) internet-draft*. draft-ietf-manet-olsrv2-19.
5. Clausen, T., & Jacquet, P. (2003). Optimised link state routing protocol (OLSR). *RFC 3626, IETF*.
6. Dohler, M., & Li, Y. (2010). *Cooperative communications - hardware, channel & PHY*. New York: Wiley.
7. Doppler, K., Redana, S., Wódczak, M., Rost, P., & Wichman, R. (2007). Dynamic resource assignment and cooperative relaying in cellular networks: Concept and performance assessment. *EURASIP Journal on Wireless Communications and Networking, 2009*, 1–14
8. Laneman, J. N., Tse, D. N. C, & Wornell, G. W. (2004). Cooperative diversity in wireless networks: Efficient protocols and outage behavior. *IEEE Transactions on Information Theory, 50*(12), 3062–3080.
9. Laneman, J. N., & Wornell, G. W. (2003). Distributed space-time-coded protocols for exploiting cooperative diversity in wireless networks. *IEEE Transactions on Information Theory, 49*(10), 2415–2425.
10. Pabst, R., Walke, B., Schultz, D. C., Herhold, P., Yanikomeroglu, H., Mukherjee, S., et al. (2004). Relay-based deployment concepts for wireless and mobile broadband radio. *IEEE Communications Magazine, 42*(9), 80–89.
11. Wódczak, M. (2007). Extended REACT - routing information enhanced algorithm for cooperative transmission. In: *16th IST Mobile & Wireless Communications Summit 2007*, Budapest, Hungary, 1–5 July 2007.
12. Wódczak, M. (2011). Aspects of cross-layer design in autonomic cooperative networking. In: *IEEE 3rd International Workshop on Cross Layer Design*, Rennes, France, 30 Nov–1 Dec 2011.
13. Wódczak, M. (2011). Autonomic cooperation in Ad-hoc environments. In: *5th International Workshop on Localised Algorithms and Protocols for Wireless Sensor Networks (LOCALGOS) in Conjunction with IEEE International Conference on Distributed Computing in Sensor Systems (DCOSS)*, Barcelona, Spain, 27–29 June 2011.
14. Wódczak, M. (2011). Autonomic cooperative networking for wireless green sensor systems. *International Journal of Sensor Networks (IJSNet), 10*(1/2), 83–93.
15. Wódczak, M. (2012). *Autonomic cooperative networking*. New York: Springer.
16. Wódczak, M., Meriem, T. B., Radier, B., Chaparadza, R., Quinn, K., Kielthy, J., et al. (2011). Standardizing a reference model and autonomic network architectures for the self-managing future internet. *IEEE Network, 25*(6), 50–56.
17. Wódczak, M., Tcholtchev, N., Vidalenc, B., & Li, Y. (2013). Design and evaluation of techniques for resilience and survivability of the routing node. *International Journal of Adaptive, Resilient and Autonomic Systems (IJARAS), 4*(4), 36–63.
18. Zimmermann, E., Herhold, P., & Fettweis, G. (2005). On the performance of cooperative relaying in wireless networks. *European Transactions on Telecommunications, 16*(1), 5–16.

# Chapter 6
# Autonomic Decision Making Entities

## 6.1 Introduction

Thus far, the vital components of the Autonomic Cooperative System Architectural Model (ACSAM), in the form of the Autonomic Cooperative Behaviour (ACB) and Autonomic Cooperative Networking Protocol (ACNP), have been outlined. In this chapter the complementary Decision Making Entities are introduced. First, the Cooperative Transmission Decision Element CT_DE is deployed on the protocol level and intended to orchestrate the Virtual Multiple Input Multiple Output based and Distributed Spatio-Temporal Block Coding enabled collaborative transmission on the Link Layer. Following the GANA assumption related to protocol simplicity, certain logic is elevated to the function level, where the Cooperation Management Decision Element CM_DE is located. Its role is to interact with the Autonomic Cooperative Networking Protocol responsible for the integration of collaborative transmission based on Distributed Spatio-Temporal Block Coding into the Multi-Point Relay station selection heuristics through the instantiation of Virtual Cooperative Sets exposing Autonomic Cooperative Behaviour. Moving up to the node level, the Cooperative Re-Routing Decision Element CR_DE is introduced able to trigger the relevant cooperative re-routing procedure well in advance and, thus, guarantee service continuity. Last but not least is the Cooperation Orchestration Decision Element CO_DE being responsible for overseeing the overall Autonomic Cooperative Behaviour related situation of the Autonomic System from the highest, network-level perspective, and, orchestrating various ACB accordingly.

## 6.2 Architectural and Conceptual Context

Given the initially introduced comprehensive architectural context, as generally sketched in Fig. 3.6, the presentation of ACSAM was performed vertically, i.e. bottom-up, placing the ACNP on top of the ACB. Such an approach was most

M. Wódczak, *Autonomic Computing Enabled Cooperative Networked Design*,
SpringerBriefs in Computer Science, DOI 10.1007/978-1-4939-0764-9_6,
© The Author(s) 2014

naturally dictated by the structure of the Open Systems Interconnection (OSI) Reference Model (RM) of a vertical orientation, too. However, putting the ACNP above the ACB would by no means suggest the two should be separate or hermetic as the OSI layers are. Quite the opposite, the Autonomic Cooperative Behaviour needs to be perceived as rather being immersed in the ACNP, mostly due to the functional interdependencies between the two. In fact, as explained in the case of the etymology and the notion of cooperation, the Autonomic Cooperative Behaviour being based on Virtual Multiple Input Multiple Output channel, Distributed Spatio-Temporal Block Coding, and Multi-Point Relay station selection heuristics spans over multiple OSI layers, starting from the Physical Layer, through the Link Layer, and up to the Network Layer. Similarly, the Autonomic Cooperative Networking Protocol is a cross-layer concept, mostly rooted in the Network Layer through the Optimised Link State Routing protocol, in the Link Layer through the integration of the DSTBC, as well as in the Physical Layer through the orchestration of VMIMO, once again with the use of ACB [10].

In the following sections both the Autonomic Cooperative Behaviour and Autonomic Cooperative Networking Protocol will be complemented by the relevant ACSAM-compliant autonomic Decision Making Elements (DMEs), devised on the basis of the rationale behind the Generic Autonomic Network Architecture (GANA) [16]. However, as visible in Fig. 6.1, the orientation of the GANA stack is horizontal which means that the concept of ACSAM will be further extended, yet in another, orthogonal direction. Looking at Fig. 6.1, one may notice, that the shape of the GANA levels of abstraction is trapezoidal and it becomes reduced towards the OSI stack. The reason for such a presentation results from the fact that from a conceptual perspective there is no obstacle for a higher level Decision Element to access the OSI layers directly.[1] In other words, the previously presented cases

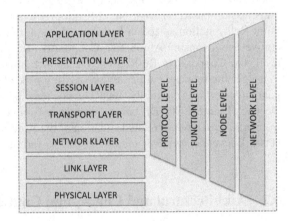

**Fig. 6.1** Architectural interactions between OSI and GANA

---

[1]It is assumed so in this book despite the fact that the acronym of Generic Autonomic Network Architecture (GANA) could potentially imply the Network Layer only, while, in fact the network

of Autonomic Cooperative Behaviour and Autonomic Cooperative Networking Protocol were outlined in such a way that the autonomic overlay was not exposed, in spite of having existed. In the former case it manifested itself through the dynamic composition of ACB in terms of the adaptability of Distributed Spatio-Temporal Block Coding, while it later one, it was related to the adaptive operation of the Multi-Point Relay station selection heuristics allowing for the dynamic allocation of Autonomic Cooperative Nodes to their respective Virtual Cooperative Sets [17].

## 6.3 Protocol Level Cooperative Transmission

In Sect. 5.2 an attempt was made to account for the difference between the notion of a Link Layer and Network Layer protocol. As it was concluded that, due to the functional and semantic differences, the proposed Autonomic Cooperative Networking Protocol (ACNP) would be more of a cross-layer solution, falling somewhere in between the two of them, yet still being a bit biased towards the Network Layer. However, when the introduction of the Cooperative Transmission Decision Element CT_DE is concerned, given the scope of the GANA abstraction related to the protocol level, it appears that a conceptual split between the Link Layer and Network Layer is mandatory, as from this viewpoint the Link Layer related part of the ACNP would be a better match for the CT_DE, after all. In other words, the cross-layering dimension of ACNP would need to be orchestrated not only by CT_DE, but also by the Cooperation Management Decision Element CM_DE, to be introduced in the following section. This way certain duality becomes conspicuous, as it is necessary to deal with the notion of a protocol in a narrow and broad context. In particular, the narrow sense CT_DE is bound to be responsible for informing the broad sense CM_DE about the necessity of involving additional intermediary Autonomic Cooperative Nodes for the needs of forming Virtual Cooperative Sets intended to contribute to the composition of the Autonomic Cooperative Behaviour in the way described below [14].

It is assumed that a two-hop collaborative transmission taking place between the source node $x$ and the destination node $n^{(2)}$ is orchestrated by the CT_DE in an Autonomic Control Loop (ACL). Moreover, the $C(n^{(2)})$ is defined as a set of channel coefficients for the radio channels between all $n$ Autonomic Cooperative Nodes, conceptually belonging to the one-hop neighbourhood $N(x)$ of the node $x$, and the destination node $n^{(2)}$ located in its two-hop neighbourhood of the said source node and denoted as $N^{(2)}(x)$ [14]. Depending on the threshold value $\beta$, the parameters of the radio links monitored in the Autonomic Control Loop, as well as any imposed policies, the CT_DE may decide that the VMIMO-based collaborative transmission, constituting the lowest level of the notion of Autonomic Cooperative

---

should be perceived as a holistic networked system featuring Autonomic Cooperative Nodes, which implement the full Open Systems Interconnection protocol stack.

Behaviour, should be assisted by three or four intermediary Autonomic Cooperative Nodes, as dictated by the $G_3$ and $G_4$ matrices chosen for this analysis. Those ACNs form a Virtual Cooperative Set denoted as $VCS(x, n^{(2)})$ and capable of encoding the received signal in a distributed manner, i.e. with the use of selected spatio-temporal block code matrix. Consequently, the $VCS(x, n^{(2)})$ may be perceived as a set or group of Autonomic Cooperative Nodes expressing the Autonomic Cooperative Behaviour through the instantiation of Distributed Spatio-Temporal Block Coding allowing for the autonomic switching between the said code matrices [1]. Most obviously, the other spatio-temporal block codes would be also applicable and the two have been chosen, as they are characterised by the same code rate of $\frac{1}{2}$ making the results directly comparable [7].

---

**Algorithm 1** Logic of CT_DE
---

1: $n = min(C(n^{(2)}))$
2: **if** $C(n^{(2)})[n] < \beta$ **then**
3:     $VCS(x, n^{(2)}) \leftarrow VCS(x, n^{(2)}) \backslash \{n\}$
4:     $DSTBC \leftarrow G_3$
5: **else**
6:     $DSTBC \leftarrow G_4$
7: **end if**

---

The logic of the CT_DE can be described as outlined in Algorithm 1. The $G_3$ mode is selected if the minimum value out of the moduli of the channel coefficients is lower than the given threshold $\beta$ [14]. As a result, one of the four allowable ACNs may no longer be included $VCS(x, n^{(2)})$, and only the three remaining ACNs are entitled to enter collaborative transmission in accordance with the $G_3$ code matrix. Otherwise, all four ACNs are used and the DSTBC operates in the $G_4$ mode [11]. In this way the worst radio link is autonomically discarded until its parameters, monitored in the Autonomic Control Loop, potentially meet the selection criterion of the CT_DE logic once again. However, should it happen so, it is necessary to keep in mind that the monitoring data may be potentially overridden by the policies imposed by a higher level Decision Making Element, such as the aforementioned CM_DE. The below evaluation results, intended to illustrate the presented case, assume the usage of a special configuration of a VMIMO[2] flat fading Rayleigh channel with a single receiving antenna at the destination node $n^{(2)}$, where the fading coefficients for each of the links between a given ACN and the Destination Node are calculated according to the modified and optimised simulation model, as to be introduced in Sect. 7.5 [18]. What is more, the power emitted by each of the actively collaborating ACNs is always normalised so that the overall transmitted power may amount to unity, while the received signal is perturbed by additive white Gaussian noise characterised by a zero mean and $N_0/2$ variance per dimension.

---

[2]Such a configuration could be also most naturally referred to as a Virtual Multiple Input Single Output (VMISO) channel.

**Fig. 6.2** Autonomic CT_DE versus Plain $G_4$ DSTBC for $\beta = 0.8$

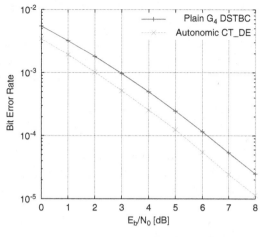

**Fig. 6.3** Autonomic CT_DT in function of $\beta$ versus $E_b/N_0$

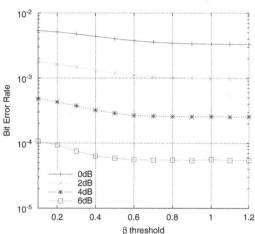

For the simulation experiment itself, always 40 million bits were transmitted and the Quadrature Phase Shift Keying (QPSK) modulation scheme was employed. The results for $\beta = 0.8$ in comparison with the reference curve for a regular $G_4$ based DSTBC are presented in Fig. 6.2, where a gain of about 1 dB is achieved. Following, the detailed results pertaining to the Bit Error Rate (BER) improvement for a specific value of the $E_b/N_0$ ratio, given a certain threshold $\beta$, are presented in Fig. 6.3. In fact, the improvement resulting from the operation of CT_DE may be observed regardless of the $E_b/N_0$ ratio, and the optimum region seems to be delimited by $\beta = 0.5$ and $\beta = 0.8$.

## 6.4    Function Level Cooperation Management

As indicated in the previous section, given the assumption in regard to the reduced complexity of the external protocols interfaced with at the protocol level of the Generic Autonomic Network Architecture abstraction, certain part of Autonomic Cooperative Networking Protocol is to be orchestrated by the CM_DE. It does not mean, however, that part of ACNP, i.e. the one related to the Network Layer, needs to be shifted to the function level. In fact, ACNP ought not to necessarily be perceived as a monolithic protocol which means that its internal and distributed entities may interface with both the autonomic overlay levels of protocol and function in accordance with the GANA nomenclature. In particular, the said entities, expected to belong with the function level, are mostly related to the two main aspects of Autonomic Cooperative Networking Protocol. Primarily, and most naturally, the interaction of the CM_DE with ACNP takes place through the adjustments to the dissemination interval of the Modified Hello messages, as well as through the adaptation of the Willingness of Autonomic Cooperative Nodes to carry and forward traffic. Consequently, the convergence time of the allocation of ACNs to the relevant Virtual Cooperative Sets can be tightly controlled, while the ACNs, characterised by Willingness of WILL_NEVER, automatically disregarded as potential Multi-Point Relays [2]. This is, in fact, related to the key aspect consisting in the control of the modified MPR station selection heuristics for the needs of guaranteeing a proper composition of Autonomic Cooperative Behaviour [12].

---

**Algorithm 2** Logic of CM_DE

---

1: $i \leftarrow 1$
2: **while** $N(x) \neq$ **do**
3:     $MPR^i(x) \leftarrow$ OLSR_MPR_HEURISTICS$(N(x))$
4:     **for all** $n \in MPR^i(x)$ **do**
5:       **for all** $n^{(2)} \in N^{(2)}(x)$ **do**
6:         **if** $neighbour(n, n^{(2)})$ **then**
7:           $j \leftarrow size(VCS(x, n^{(2)})) - 1$
8:           **while** $j \geq 0$ **and** $P^{n^{(2)}}_{VCS(x,n^{(2)})[j]} < P^{n^{(2)}}_n$ **do**
9:             $VCS(x, n^{(2)})[j+1] \leftarrow VCS(x, n^{(2)})[j]$
10:             $j \leftarrow j - 1$
11:           **end while**
12:           $VCS(x, n^{(2)})[j+1] \leftarrow n$
13:         **end if**
14:       **end for**
15:     **end for**
16:     $N(x) \leftarrow N(x) \backslash MPR^i(x)$
17:     $i \leftarrow i + 1$
18: **end while**

---

The relevant description of the logic of the CM_DE related to the composition of Autonomic Cooperative Behaviour with the use of the classic MPR selection heuristics of the OLSR protocol is provided in Algorithm 2 [8]. In particular, it is assumed that all neighbours $n$ characterised by a zero degree are removed by the source node $x$ from the one-hop neighbourhood $N(x)$ before the algorithm is executed. Following, the said MPR station selection heuristics is performed iteratively over the set $N(x)$, until all the ACNs, potentially meeting the selection criteria, are assigned to distinct $MPR^i(x)$ subsets. In fact, it is assumed that all the ACNs are able to expose Autonomic Cooperative Behaviour and, thus, are capable of forming Virtual Cooperative Sets. Consequently, each iteration results in an additional subset of MPRs, i.e. secondary, ternary, and so on, denoted as $MPR^i(x)$, while, at the same time, all the ACNs contained in such a subset are distributed among the most relevant Virtual Cooperative Sets (VCSs). Those VCSs are denoted as $VCS(x, n^{(2)})$ and are capable of providing collaborative transmission between the source node $x$ and the destination node $n^{(2)}$, where $n^{(2)}$ belongs to the two-hop symmetric neighbourhood of $x$. As a result, any intermediate node $n$ can be included in more than one VCSs so that not only all the intermediate ACNs are assigned, but also additional redundancy is introduced to the classic MPR station selection mechanism. This redundancy can be utilised autonomically in case there are a lot of very sudden changes in the network topology, when those additional $MPR^i(x)$ can be taken into account adaptively.

| 1 | R_dest_addr | R_next_addr | R_dist | R_iface_addr |      |      |
|---|-------------|-------------|--------|--------------|------|------|
| 1 | R_dest_addr | R_next_addr | R_dist | R_iface_addr | addr |      |
| 1 | R_dest_addr | R_next_addr | R_dist | R_iface_addr | addr | addr |
| 2 | R_dest_addr | R_next_addr | R_dist | R_iface_addr | addr |      |
| 3 | R_dest_addr | R_next_addr | R_dist | R_iface_addr |      | addr |
| ... | ... | ... | ... | ... | addr |      |
| K | R_dest_addr | R_next_addr | R_dist | R_iface_addr |      |      |

**Fig. 6.4**  ACNP routing table

In is crucial to note, however, that the availability of additional power level information conveyed within the Extended Link Code of the Modified Hello message makes it possible to place the ACNs selected as MPRs in $VCS(x, n^{(2)})$ at the positions corresponding to the power level at which they are heard by the Destination Node. As a result, the first ACNs in a Virtual Cooperative Set are the ones of the ability to provide the best collaborative connectivity to the DN. In fact, such a collaborative connectivity requires proper packet routing. While, in general, should the Network Layer send a packet to a Destination Node of an IP[3] address of the value R_dest_addr, it uses the IP address of the value R_next_addr and requests

---

[3]Internet Protocol (IP) is meant here.

the Link Layer to send the said packet, with the aid of a MAC[4] Layer frame, to a MAC address[5] corresponding to this R_next_addr IP address. However, in the case of ACNP a packet must be transmitted concurrently over all the ACNs belonging to a given VCS [14]. This issue may be addressed by associating an additional routing table with each column of the spatio-temporal block code matrix, which leads to a multidimensional routing table, as depicted in Fig. 6.4. The operation of CM_DE,

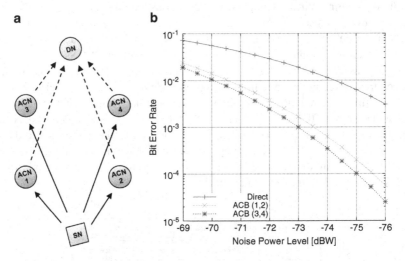

**Fig. 6.5**  ACNP scenario and results for CM_DE

able to orchestrate the composition of ACB and perform autonomic switching to the best VCS, is presented in Fig. 6.5. As the scenario outlined in Fig. 6.5a contains two VCSs, each of the size of two, it suffices for ACNP to maintain a two-dimensional routing table only. According to the information stored in the ACB Selector Set, as outlined in Sect. 5.5, one entry will be included in the first routing table, whereas the other entry will go to the second routing table. In other words, should the CM_DE decide that the SN send a packet to the DN in a collaborative manner,[6] both routing tables need to be checked. As a result, the protocol level CT_DE might be requested to orchestrate the ACB with the use of the $G_2$ based DSTBC, but the decision on which VCS to use will be made by the CM_DE. In particular, the distance from the SN to each of the nodes forming $VCS(1,2)$ and $VCS(3,4)$ is equal to 10 and 24 m, respectively, while the SN is located 29 m from the DN. The velocity of ACNs ranges from 0 to 1.4 m/s and a LOS channel model of the path-loss $L(d)$ is assumed (6.1) [4]:

---

[4]Medium Access Control (MAC) is meant here.

[5]Resolved with the aid of the Address Resolution Protocol (ARP) [6].

[6]Such a decision might be imposed, for example, by the Quality of Service (QoS) requirements.

$$L(d) = 13.4 \log_{10}(d) + 36.9 \quad [\text{dB}], \tag{6.1}$$

where $5 \, \text{m} < d < 29 \, \text{m}$ represents the distance, the shadow fading standard deviation $\sigma$ is equal to $1.3 \, \text{dB}$. Additionally, the SN is assumed to transmit with the average power equal to $200 \, \text{mW}$, while the gain of its antenna is equal to $8 \, \text{dBi}$. The ACNs are characterised by the corresponding parameters of $200 \, \text{mW}$ and $0 \, \text{dBi}$, respectively. The QPSK modulation scheme is assumed and the noise figure introduced by the radio frequency chain is equal to $7 \, \text{dB}$ [14]. The simulations were performed in the presence of a zero mean additive white Gaussian noise characterised by the power level $N$ expressed in dBW. Always 100 million bits were transmitted and, as visible in Fig. 6.5a, the $VCS(3,4) = \{3,4\}$ performed best.

## 6.5  Node Level Cooperative Re-Routing

Looking from the higher level perspective, there might appear a need for reconfiguration of the already on-going collaborative and non-collaborative transmissions on the basis of additional information, which might be coming from both the Resilience and Survivability Decision Element RS_DE and the Fault Management Decision Element FM_DE [13]. In particular, the Decision Making Entities of an Autonomic System might be able to infer certain imminent failure from the root causes as analysed by the FM_DE and employ the RM_DE to orchestrate the remediation action. The CR_DE may be indispensable in such a context as it might impose the instantiation of collaborative transmission on the CM_DE even in the case where a non-collaborative transmission would normally suffice. In other words, should a failure be to occur, the CR_DE could attempt to avoid the typical switching to alternative paths after it happens, as advocated for by the legacy Fast Re-Routing (FRR), by orchestrating the Autonomic Cooperative Behaviour among ACNs well beforehand. To this end, the CM_DE may be used together with ACNP for the purposes of routing packets over multiple collaborative paths. One should note, however, that such a multi-path operation cannot be confused with the Equal Cost Multipath Protocol (ECMP) [5]. In particular, while, in general, the ECMP aims to help with load balancing, the ACNP gains from increased robustness of the Distributed Spatio-Temporal Block Coding enabled VMIMO transmission.

Looking at the scenario, Fig. 6.6a depicts the legacy approach to Fast Re-Routing (FRR), where the packet stream between the SN and the DN would be routed over ACN2 before FRR has been engaged. Should there appear a failure of any of the link 1, link 2, or ACN2, in particular, one of the readily available and pre-computed back-up paths would be used instead almost instantly. In this very case, there would be the following optional paths available formed of the links (3, 4, 5), (3, 6), or (7, 8). One should note that only one of them could be used in the typical Fast Re-Routing approach. This process can be obviously enhanced with the proper application of Autonomic Cooperative Behaviour, because the CR_DE does no need

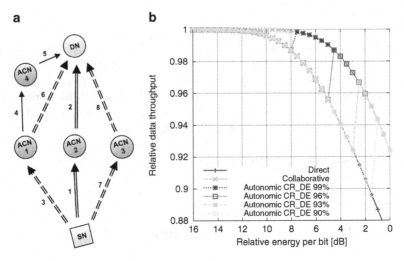

**Fig. 6.6** FRR scenario and results for CR_DE

---

**Algorithm 3** Logic of CR_DE

---

1: **if** $(\mathbf{BER}(x,n) < \theta$ **or** $\mathbf{BER}(n,n^2) < \theta)$ **then**
2:     **if** $VCS(x,n^{(2)}) \neq \emptyset$ **then**
3:         $\mathbf{ACB}(VCS(x,n^{(2)}))$
4:     **else**
5:         $\mathbf{FRR}(x,n^{(2)})$
6:     **end if**
7: **end if**

---

to wait with the exploitation of the alternative pat or paths until a link failure has occurred, as described in Algorithm 3 [14]. In particular, the links between the source node $x$ and the one-hop neighbour $n$, playing the role of an ACN, as well as between the said ACN and the destination node $n^{(2)}$ need to be checked for Bit Error Rate (BER) compliance. Depending on whether both, or just one of them, may offer the requested transmission quality, further steps are undertaken. And, thus, the CR_DE needs to check whether there exist any group of ACNs that would be able to form a VCS between the SN and the DN. The VCS sets are provided, in turn, directly by the CM_DE, which interacts with the Autonomic Cooperative Networking Protocol, and are used to support the CR_DE in orchestrating the task of Cooperative Re-Routing (CRR) [14]. Consequently, it suffices to verify whether a given VCS is valid and, should it be so, the ACB may be exercised. Otherwise, the operation of the legacy FRR would need to be commenced.

The performance of the CR_DE was evaluated as outlined in Fig. 6.6b. The AWGN channel was used together with the QPSK modulation and each time 10 million bits were transmitted. The obtained curves illustrate that for a given BER threshold, of 90, 93, 96, and 99 percent, respectively, the CR_DE may autonomically switch from the non-collaborative transmission, performed with the use of a singular

ACN, to the collaborative one supported by a group of ACNs forming a VCS and, thus, instantiating Autonomic Cooperative Behaviour. In other words, this way a Signal-to-Interference-plus-Noise Ratio (SINR) gain may be observed, allowing to avoid the necessity of choosing another path, as it would be normally the case for FRR. Quite the contrary, it is possible to maintain the connection over a diversified set of collaborative paths, despite some problems with a single link.

## 6.6   Network Level Cooperation Orchestration

Last but not least is the network level Cooperation Orchestration Decision Element CO_DE. Once again, similarly to the protocol level of GANA abstraction, also in this case the nomenclature might pose certain dose of uncertainty. Clearly, such a statement is conditioned by the fact that the notion of the network level[7] should not be confused with the OSI RM Network Layer. In the case of GANA, the network level is an abstract entity formed by selected nodes only having the capability of implementing it. The reason for such an approach is that a physical device of the name or functionality of a network does not even exist. In fact, while the OSI Network Layer generally pertains to the relevant networking protocols and addressing schemes, the GANA network level, quite the contrary, seems to be the incarnation of the perception of the entire networked system. In particular, the orchestration of such a system, in terms of the instantiation of Autonomic Cooperative Behaviour on the network level, is the domain of the CO_DE, whose logic is outlined in the form of a sequence diagram, as depicted in Fig. 6.7. The need for the composition of ACB by the network level Decision Element might result from the fact that the Autonomic Cooperative Networking Protocol, being based on the MPR station selection heuristics, may not be able to put an ACN of interest into a Virtual Cooperative Set because, for example, that ACN decided autonomically to set its willingness to carry and forward traffic to WILL_NEVER on one of its interfaces.

The sequence diagram of Fig. 6.7 describes a case where a non-collaborative transmission is not possible and, for the above reasons, the SN needs to additionally request the ACN2 to enter Autonomic Cooperative Behaviour in the first place, while normally the ACNs would be listed in the Link Message in a reverse order.

Such a scheme was investigated in the ACN layout depicted in Fig. 6.8, where four different groups of ACNs are arranged arbitrarily in a more or less circular manner [15]. In particular, this indoor scenario consists of one floor of a height of 3 m in a building, where two corridors of dimensions of $5 \times 100$ m and 40 rooms of dimensions of $10 \times 10$ m are located [9]. A fixed modulation and coding scheme

---

[7]Mostly for the reason of emphasising the distinction between GANA and OSI, the layers of OSI are capitalised throughout the whole book, while the levels of GANA are not. The capitalisation is not intended to indicate any precedence, however.

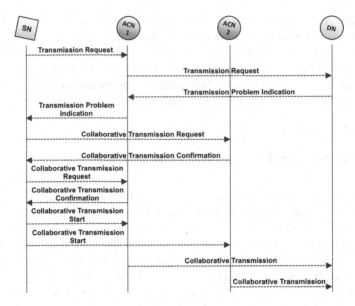

**Fig. 6.7** Logic of CO_DE

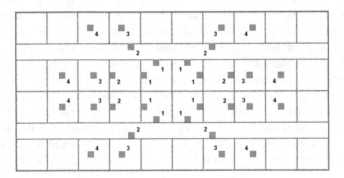

**Fig. 6.8** Layout A

was employed based on a QPSK modulation and (4, 5, 7) convolutional code. The AWGN channel was assumed together with either the A1 Line of Sight (LOS) (6.2) or A1 Non Line-of-Sight (NLOS) (6.3) radio propagation model, as defined below [3].

$$PL_{LOS}[dB] = 18.7\log_{10}(d) + 46.8 + \sigma, \tag{6.2}$$

where $d$ denotes the distance in meters between the SN and the DN and $\sigma$ represents the standard deviation of shadow fading and is equal to 3 dB.

$$PL_{NLOS}[dB] = 20.0\log_{10}(d) + 46.4 + 5n_w + \sigma, \tag{6.3}$$

where $n_w$ denotes the number of walls between the transmitter and the receiver and $\sigma$ is equal to 6 dB. The relative throughput for each of the circular configurations from A.1 through A.4 is presented in Fig. 6.9.

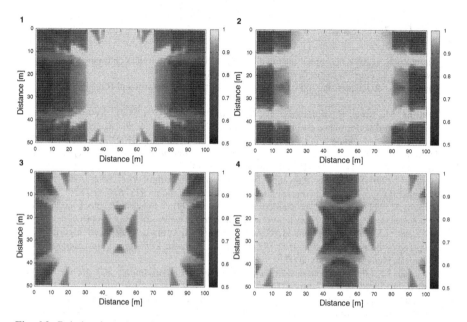

**Fig. 6.9** Relative throughput for layouts A.1–A.4

## 6.7 Conclusion

In this chapter, the relevant Decision Making Entities are introduced bottom-up. First, the protocol level Cooperative Transmission Decision Element CT_DE was presented as being responsible for orchestrating the Virtual Multiple Input Multiple Output based and DSTBC-enabled collaborative transmission at the Link Layer. Following, certain logic was elevated to the function level, where the Cooperation Management Decision Element CM_DE was placed and intended to interact with the Autonomic Cooperative Networking Protocol and, thus, integrate the Distributed Spatio-Temporal Block Coding based collaborative transmission into the Multi-Point Relay station selection heuristics through the instantiation of Virtual Cooperative Sets exposing Autonomic Cooperative Behaviour. Moving up to the node level, the Cooperative Re-Routing Decision Element CR_DE was deployed as being able to trigger the relevant cooperative re-routing procedure well in advance and, thus, guarantee service continuity. Last but not least the Cooperation Orchestration Decision Element CO_DE was presented to be responsible for overseeing the overall Autonomic Cooperative Behaviour related situation of the Autonomic System from the highest, network-level perspective.

# References

1. Alamouti, S. (1998). A simple transmit diversity technique for wireless communications. *IEEE Journal on Selected Areas in Communications, 16*(8), 1451–1458.
2. Clausen, T., & Jacquet, P. (2003). Optimised link state routing protocol (OLSR). *RFC 3626, IETF*.
3. Dottling, M., Irmer, R., Kalliojarvi, K., & Rouquette-Leveil, S. (2009). System model, test scenarios, and performance evaluation. In: M. Dottling, W. Mohr, & A. Osseiran (Eds.), *Radio technologies and concepts for IMT-Advanced*. New York: Wiley. ISBN: 978-0-470-74763-6.
4. Dottling, M., Mohr, W., & Osseiran, A. (2009). *Radio technologies and concepts for IMT-advanced*. New York: Wiley. ISBN: 978-0-470-74763-6.
5. Hopps, C. (2004). Analysis of an equal-cost multi-path algorithm. *RFC 2992, IETF*.
6. Plummer, D. C. (1982). An ethernet address resolution protocol. *RFC 826, IETF*.
7. Tarokh, V., Jafarkhani, H., & Calderbank, A. R. (1999). Space-time block codes from orthogonal designs. *IEEE Transactions on Information Theory, 45*(5), 1456–1467.
8. Wódczak, M. (2007). Extended REACT - routing information enhanced algorithm for cooperative transmission. In: *16th IST Mobile & Wireless Communications Summit 2007*, Budapest, Hungary, 1–5 July 2007.
9. Wódczak, M. (2008). Cooperative relaying in an indoor environment. *ICT Mobile Summit*, Stockholm, Sweden, 10–12 June 2008.
10. Wódczak, M. (2011). Aspects of cross-layer design in autonomic cooperative networking. In: *IEEE 3rd International Workshop on Cross Layer Design*, Rennes, France, 30 Nov–1 Dec 2011.
11. Wódczak, M. (2011). Autonomic cooperation in ad-hoc environments. In: *5th International Workshop on Localised Algorithms and Protocols for Wireless Sensor Networks (LOCALGOS) in Conjunction with IEEE International Conference on Distributed Computing in Sensor Systems (DCOSS)*, Barcelona, Spain, 27–29 June 2011.
12. Wódczak, M. (2011). Autonomic cooperative networking for wireless green sensor systems. *International Journal of Sensor Networks (IJSNet), 10*(1/2), 83–93.
13. Wódczak, M. (2011). Resilience aspects of autonomic cooperative communications in context of cloud networking. In: *IEEE 1st Symposium on Network Cloud Computing and Applications*, Toulouse, France, 21–23 Nov 2011.
14. Wódczak, M. (2012). *Autonomic cooperative networking*. New York: Springer.
15. Wódczak, M. (2012). Convergence aspects of autonomic cooperative networks. *International Journal of Information Technology and Web Engineering (IJITWE), 6*(4), 51–62.
16. Wódczak, M., Meriem, T. B., Radier, B., Chaparadza, R., Quinn, K., Kielthy, J., et al. (2011). Standardizing a reference model and autonomic network architectures for the self-managing future internet. *IEEE Network, 25*(6), 50–56.
17. Wódczak, M., Szott, S., & Chaparadza, R. (2013). Autonomic cooperative behaviour in ETSI AFI scenario for autonomicity enabled Ad-hoc and mesh network architecture. In: *5th IEEE MENS at GLOBECOM 2013*, Atlanta, Georgia, USA, 9–13 Dec 2013.
18. Zheng, Y. R. & Xiao, C. (2003). Simulation models with correct statistical properties for Rayleigh fading channels. *IEEE Transactions on Communications, 51*(6), 920–928.

# Chapter 7
# Implementation and Simulation Environment

## 7.1 Introduction

Following all the previous chapters, where the key components of the Autonomic Cooperative System Architectural Model (ACSAM) in the form of the Autonomic Cooperative Behaviour (ACB) and Autonomic Cooperative Networking Protocol (ACNP) were outlined, this chapter aims to provide certain dose of insight into the practical side of the proposed concept, most obviously related to the implementation and simulation aspects. To this end, first of all the architecture of the developed simulator is introduced, which, in fact, sheds additional light on the mutual relations and interactions between the layers of the implemented protocol stack and the levels of abstraction containing the relevant Decision Elements (DEs). Following, the operational aspects of the functioning of the protocol itself are presented in the context of explaining the pertinent encapsulation mechanisms. Based on this, the very concept of multi-threading with the use of the Java programming language is discussed not only to highlight the most important assumptions, but, additionally, to show its direct relevance to and the gain from the notion of Autonomic Cooperative Behaviour (ACB) when realised properly with the use of multiple threads. This part is further complemented with the mathematical analysis of the reception of the Distributed Spatio-Temporal Block Coding (DSTBC) processed signals. Finally, the parameters of the assumed scenario are described together with the corresponding layouts of Autonomic Cooperative Nodes (ACNs), and the relevant reference simulation results are provided.

## 7.2 Simulator Architecture

The architecture of the simulator is, in fact, a very detailed instantiation of the overall Autonomic Cooperative System Architectural Model (ACSAM) proposed in this book, as outlined in Fig. 7.1. It directly builds on top of the sketch of the architectural

M. Wódczak, *Autonomic Computing Enabled Cooperative Networked Design*,
SpringerBriefs in Computer Science, DOI 10.1007/978-1-4939-0764-9_7,
© The Author(s) 2014

interactions between OSI and GANA introduced in the previous chapter in Fig. 6.1, where the orthogonality of the two was clearly underlined. In this section, however, there generalities of the OSI and the GANA are replaced with the specific workings of the ACSAM. In particular, a proprietary protocol stack is employed where the following layers are specified: Physical Layer PHY_Layer, Link Layer LNK_Layer, Network Layer NET_Layer, and a joint Application-Presentation-Session-Transport Layer APST_Layer. Even though the stack is composed of four layers, thus leaning towards the Transmission Control Protocol/Internet Protocol (TCP/IP) one, functionally it is still more closely related to and stems from the reduction of the OSI RM. In particular, the most top layer encompasses the four highest OSI layers, which means that the Presentation Layer and Session Layer are not exposed in any particular way, which highly resembles the TCP/IP approach [6]. Looking towards the GANA evolved Decision Making Entities, in turn, the four levels of abstraction are filled with their corresponding Cooperative Transmission Decision Element, Cooperation Management Decision Element, Cooperative Re-Routing Decision Element, and Cooperation Orchestration Decision Element.

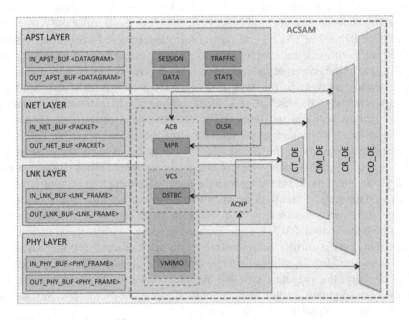

**Fig. 7.1** Implementation architecture

As visible in Fig. 7.1, the implemented instantiation of the ACSAM follows the design assumptions and spans over both the introduced protocol layers and levels of abstraction. In particular, the Cooperative Transmission Decision Element CT_DE interfaces directly with the DSTBC module only, yet DSTBC goes hand-in-hand with the Virtual Multiple Input Multiple Output module [1]. It means that, even though VMIMO belongs with the Physical Layer, its functional correspondence with DSTBC makes the two modules constitute jointly a Virtual Cooperative Set. Going further, such a VCS incorporates the MPR station selection heuristics of the OLSR protocol to establish Autonomic Cooperative Behaviour [17]. One should note, however, that while the MPR station selection heuristics is managed by the Cooperation Management Decision Element CM_DE, the overall ACB is already interfaced with by the Cooperative Re-Routing Decision Element for resilience and survivability, as well as fault-management related purposes, already signalled in Sect. 6.5 [12]. Following, there is the Autonomic Cooperative Networking Protocol itself linking all the above-mentioned components but residing across the Network Layer and the Link Layer only [10]. As such, ACNP is overlooked by the Cooperation Orchestration Decision Element CO_DE. The global picture of the Autonomic Cooperative System Architectural Model is complemented by the modules of the APST Layer, mostly responsible for the generation of data bits and traffic modelling with some elements of session maintenance, as well as a statistics and results analysis related module.

## 7.3   Operational Aspects

Due to the complexity of the proposed Autonomic Cooperative System Archi-tectural Model, not to mention the need for certain dose of cross-layering, the Autonomic Cooperative Nodes do not communicate directly, but by means of the protocol stack only, as depicted in Fig. 7.2. Such an approach not only guarantees

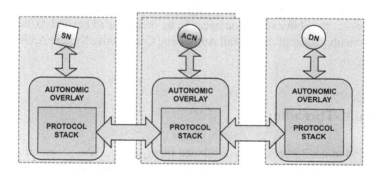

**Fig. 7.2**  Interaction over protocol stack

the realism of simulation but, in fact, it appears indispensable for the development o a fully-fledged system. In particular, for the purposes of having the collaborative transmission over wireless links organised properly, a simplified CSMA/CA access method is implemented at the Link Layer. What is more, as each Autonomic Cooperative Node is bound to perform the operation of link sensing, neighbour discovery, and Autonomic Cooperative Behaviour composition, the relevant control messages of the OLSR-based ACNP protocol are issued at the Network Layer by being first encapsulated into OLSR Packets, and, then, into UDP[1] Datagrams [11]. Similarly, the application data are loaded into Datagrams at the APST Layer, and, then, further encapsulated into UDP Datagrams at the Network Layer, where the routing mechanisms are also going on. Following, the UDP datagrams are encapsulated into IP Packets and, in the case of containing control data, they are disseminated to all the neighbours for the purposes of link sensing and neighbour discovery, whereas in the case of containing application data, they are routed to the specific destination as indicated by the routing table.

Nevertheless, due to the nature of the wireless transmission medium, the data packets transmitted by a Source Node to its Destination Node, located two hops away, are heard not only by the intermediate ACNs, potentially intended to instantiate ACB, but also by the other neighbours. However, those ACNs which are not eventually pre-selected to collaborate, silently discard the received frames. This operation is performed at the Link Layer which is responsible for coding, decoding, encapsulation of the packets coming from the Network Layer in the Link Layer frames LNK_Frame, as well as the physical addressing, making the communication with the specified one-hop neighbour or neighbours possible. Finally, each LNK_Frame is encapsulated in the Physical Layer frame PHY_Frame and, after having been modulated, it is physically transmitted over the radio channel, additionally making it subject to impairments and distortion. The dynamic composition of Autonomic Cooperative Behaviour with the use of Network Layers routines, and the cross-layer Autonomic Cooperative Networking Protocol in particular, is intended to minimise the likelihood of the occurrence of any such undesirable effects, thus making the process of communication possibly efficient and uninterrupted [15]. As the protocol stack is implemented by every single node of the network, the above operation needs to be orchestrated beyond ACNP which is obtained with the aid of the overall Autonomic Cooperative System Architectural Model.

## 7.4   Multi-Threading

The simulation environment was developed purely in the Java programming language as a multi-threaded application where the class AutonomicCooperativeNode extends a Java Swing class defining a graphical object, a JButton in particular, and, at the same time, it implements the Callable[2] interface for the purposes of multi-threading, as illustrated in Listing 7.1 [4]. This way not only is parallel computation enabled but highly efficient visualisation is possible, as already depicted in Fig. 6.8, where all the ACNs may be mobile, obviously depending on the

---

[1] User Datagram Protocol (UDP) is meant here.

[2] The Runnable interface would be also an option but not the extension of the class Thread as already the JButton is extended and Java does not support multiple inheritance.

requirements of a given scenario. It is so as all the methods and properties inherent in the JButton class are instantly available for further exploitation. On the one hand, it allows for a dynamic repositioning so necessary for the visualisation of the said mobility of an instantiation of a given AutonomicCooperativeNode being, in fact, an element of the Graphical User Interface (GUI). On the other hand, thanks to assuming this type of an approach, also the obtaining of certain simulation-related parameters of such an object is clearly straightforward, as, through inheritance, the AutonomicCooperativeNode derives from the aforementioned JButton, after all [3]. However, not only are the objects of the AutonomicCooperativeNode class running as Java threads. In fact, all the other objects such as the specific layers of the protocol stack, together with the Decision Making Entities of the distinct abstraction levels, are also running as threads for increased performance.

**Listing 7.1** AutonomicCooperativeNode as threaded JButton

```
public class AutonomicCooperativeNode extends JButton
    implements Callable<String> {

    ...

}
```

Going further into the details, the assumed simulation method capitalises on the emulation of a conceptual interaction of virtual processes, enhanced with multi-threading [16]. Normally, all the created objects could be perceived as such processes which are scheduled on an agenda according to the global system time, and, then, executed one by one to perform their tasks and exercise the related interactions. However, given the existence of Autonomic Cooperative Nodes, such an approach would be computationally inefficient due to the parallelised nature of the simulated system. It would be so especially because of the current availability of advanced computing systems featuring multiple Central Processing Units (CPUs), each of at least several cores, whereby every single core may be capable of using the Hyper-Threading Technology (HTT). In the presented case it is additionally assumed that all the Autonomic Cooperative Nodes, being part of the Autonomic Cooperative Behaviour composed by the Autonomic Cooperative Networking Protocol, need to be run in parallel. Such a functionality may be obtained through a joint triggering of all such ACNs given a proper maintenance and overseeing of the resulting multi-threaded setup is taken care of. As a result, not only is the efficiency of the instantiation of the Autonomic Cooperative System Architectural Model improved but the parallel execution of ACNs integrates very well conceptually with the very idea of Autonomic Cooperative Behaviour, especially when perceived from the viewpoint of Distributed Spatio-Temporal Block Coding.

## 7.5 Distributed Spatio-Temporal Block Coding

The proper simulation requires a relevantly accurate modelling of the ACB through DSTBC over a VMIMO channel. Such a functionality is obtained through the application of a flat Rayleigh fading, characterised by the lack of correlation among the wireless links formed between any of the ACNs belonging with a given Virtual Cooperative Set and their pertinent Destination Node. In particular, the fading coefficients are calculated according to a sum-of-sinusoids statistical simulation model being advantageous because the autocorrelation and cross-correlation functions of the quadrature components, as well as the autocorrelation function of the complex envelope of the fading process given by (7.1), where $X_c(t)$ is defined as (7.2) and $X_s(t)$ is defined as (7.3), match the desired ones even if the number of sinusoids is solely a figure [18]:

$$X(t) = X_c(t) + jX_s(t), \qquad (7.1)$$

$$X_c(t) = \frac{2}{\sqrt{K}} \sum_{k=1}^{K} \cos(\varphi_k) \cos(\omega_d t \cos \alpha_k + \phi), \qquad (7.2)$$

$$X_s(t) = \frac{2}{\sqrt{K}} \sum_{k=1}^{K} \sin(\varphi_k) \cos(\omega_d t \cos \alpha_k + \phi). \qquad (7.3)$$

The $\alpha_k$ parameter, in turn, visible in the above equations is defined as (7.4):

$$\alpha_n = \frac{2\pi k - \pi + \theta}{4K}, \qquad k = 1, 2, \ldots, K, \qquad (7.4)$$

under the assumption that the random variables denoted by $\theta$, $\phi$, and $\varphi_k$ are statistically independent and uniformly distributed over the range of $[-\pi, \pi)$ for all the values of $k$. This model can be immediately used for the purposes of generating multiple uncorrelated fading waveforms for Virtual Multiple Input Multiple Output (VMIMO) channels making it directly applicable to the investigated Autonomic Cooperative System Architectural Model [18]. In particular, for increased computational efficiency, the general form of the decision metric, previously defined as (4.11), needs to be modified appropriately [7], so that for the $G_2$ spatio-temporal block code, it can be re-written as (7.5):

$$\sum_{j=1}^{M} \left( \left| r_1^j - h_{1,j} s_1 - h_{2,j} s_2 \right|^2 + \left| r_2^j + h_{1,j} s_2^* - h_{2,j} s_1^* \right|^2 \right) \qquad (7.5)$$

In general, a maximum-likelihood detection algorithm would aim to find the minimum value of such a metric for all the possible combinations of $s_1$ and $s_2$. In fact, the expression (7.5) may be rearranged so that the components independent of the code words could be disregarded [14]. Consequently, the minimisation problem becomes equivalent to finding the minimum of the following formula (7.6) [7]:

$$
|s_1|^2 \sum_{j=1}^{M} \sum_{i=1}^{2} |h_{i,j}|^2 - \sum_{j=1}^{M} \left[ r_1^j h_{1,j}^* s_1^* + \left( r_1^j \right)^* h_{1,j} s_1 + r_2^j h_{2,j}^* s_1 + \left( r_2^j \right)^* h_{2,j} s_1^* \right] +
$$
$$
+ |s_2|^2 \sum_{j=1}^{M} \sum_{i=1}^{2} |h_{i,j}|^2 - \sum_{j=1}^{M} \left[ r_1^j h_{2,j}^* s_2^* + \left( r_1^j \right)^* h_{2,j} s_2 - r_2^j h_{1,j}^* s_2 - \left( r_2^j \right)^* h_{1,j} s_2^* \right]
$$

(7.6)

Such a mathematical expression, in turn, may be perceived as composed of two parts, the first of them being exclusively the function of $s_1$, while the second one being exclusively the function of $s_2$. As a result, it is possible to conclude that the total value of this metric is minimum, when each of its aforementioned two components is minimum. Finally, the metric for the $G_2$ code can be written as (7.7) [7]:

$$
\left| \sum_{j=1}^{m} R_j - s \right|^2 + \left( -1 + \sum_{j=1}^{m} \sum_{i=1}^{2} |h_{i,j}|^2 \right) |s|^2 ,
$$

(7.7)

where for $s = s_1$ and $s = s_2$ the signal $R_j$, received by the antenna[3] $j$, is given by (7.8) and (7.9), respectively:

$$
R_j = r_1^j h_{1,j}^* + (r_2^j)^* h_{2,j} ,
$$

(7.8)

$$
R_j = r_1^j h_{2,j}^* - (r_2^j)^* h_{1,j} .
$$

(7.9)

Similarly, the metric for the $G_3$ code can be then written as (7.10) [7]:

$$
\left| \sum_{j=1}^{m} R_j - s \right|^2 + \left( -1 + 2 \sum_{j=1}^{m} \sum_{i=1}^{3} |h_{i,j}|^2 \right) |s|^2 ,
$$

(7.10)

where for $s = s_1$, $s = s_2$, $s = s_3$, and $s = s_4$ the signal $R_j$, received by antenna $j$, is given by (7.11), (7.12), (7.13), and (7.14), respectively:

$$
R_j = r_1^j h_{1,j}^* + r_2^j h_{2,j}^* + r_3^j h_{3,j}^* + (r_5^j)^* h_{1,j} + (r_6^j)^* h_{2,j} + (r_7^j)^* h_{3,j} ,
$$

(7.11)

$$
R_j = r_1^j h_{2,j}^* - r_2^j h_{1,j}^* + r_4^j h_{3,j}^* + (r_5^j)^* h_{2,j} - (r_6^j)^* h_{1,j} + (r_8^j)^* h_{3,j} ,
$$

(7.12)

---

[3]In general, such an antenna could be an element of a Multi-Element Array (MEA), either fixed or mobile, or be equivalent to an ACN, should it be equipped with a single antenna only.

$$R_j = r_1^j h_{3,j}^* - r_3^j h_{1,j}^* - r_4^j h_{2,j}^* + (r_5^j)^* h_{3,j} - (r_7^j)^* h_{1,j} - (r_8^j)^* h_{2,j}, \qquad (7.13)$$

$$R_j = -r_2^j h_{3,j}^* + r_3^j h_{2,j}^* - r_4^j h_{1,j}^* - (r_6^j)^* h_{3,j} + (r_7^j)^* h_{2,j} - (r_8^j)^* h_{1,j}. \qquad (7.14)$$

Finally, the metric for the $G_4$ code can be expressed as (7.15) [7]:

$$\left| \sum_{j=1}^{m} R_j - s \right|^2 + \left( -1 + 2 \sum_{j=1}^{m} \sum_{i=1}^{4} |h_{i,j}|^2 \right) |s|^2, \qquad (7.15)$$

where for $s = s_1$, $s = s_2$, $s = s_3$, and $s = s_4$ the signal $R_j$, received by antenna $j$, is given by (7.16), (7.17), (7.18), and (7.19)[4], respectively:

$$R_j = r_1^j h_{1,j}^* + r_2^j h_{2,j}^* + r_3^j h_{3,j}^* + r_4^j h_{4,j}^* + (r_5^j)^* h_{1,j} + (r_6^j)^* h_{2,j} + (r_7^j)^* h_{3,j} + (r_8^j)^* h_{4,j}, \qquad (7.16)$$

$$R_j = r_1^j h_{2,j}^* - r_2^j h_{1,j}^* - r_3^j h_{4,j}^* + r_4^j h_{3,j}^* + (r_5^j)^* h_{2,j} - (r_6^j)^* h_{1,j} - (r_7^j)^* h_{4,j} + (r_8^j)^* h_{3,j}, \qquad (7.17)$$

$$R_j = r_1^j h_{3,j}^* + r_2^j h_{4,j}^* - r_3^j h_{1,j}^* - r_4^j h_{2,j}^* + (r_5^j)^* h_{3,j} + (r_6^j)^* h_{4,j} - (r_7^j)^* h_{1,j} - (r_8^j)^* h_{2,j}, \qquad (7.18)$$

$$R_j = r_1^j h_{4,j}^* - r_2^j h_{3,j}^* + r_3^j h_{2,j}^* - r_4^j h_{1,j}^* + (r_5^j)^* h_{4,j} - (r_6^j)^* h_{3,j} + (r_7^j)^* h_{2,j} - (r_8^j)^* h_{1,j}. \qquad (7.19)$$

## 7.6  Scenario and Evaluation

While the simulator is capable of employing various scenarios, the indoor one introduced in the previous chapter is of special interest, as it allows for the analysis of different layouts. In particular, in this section the Layout A, presented previously in Fig. 6.8, is complemented with additional layouts B and C, as outlined in Fig. 7.3 and Fig. 7.4, respectively, where different positioning schemes of ACNs are denoted by the numbers placed next to them. In general, this scenario comprises 40 rooms of the dimensions 10 m x 10 m each, with two corridors of the dimensions 5 m x 100 m in between them [9]. Such a set-up is assumed to be arranged as a floor

---

[4]When implementing this metric, the author of this book noticed that the formula given in [7] is erroneous and so is the one given in [8] on page 107. This error does not exist in [5], however, one should note that all the $G_4$ metrics provided therein also contain a typo and are written, as if they were pertaining to a code matrix composed of 3 columns (see index $i$ on pages 87-88), whereas this code was obviously designed for 4 transmitting antennae [14].

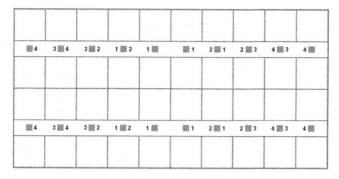

**Fig. 7.3** Layout B

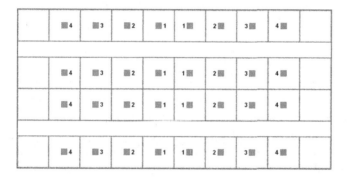

**Fig. 7.4** Layout C

of the height of 3 m located in a building [2]. All this makes the scenario highly demanding and specific, as the transmitted signals are continuously subject to rather a severe distortion being induced by the existence of numerous separating walls, acting as obstacles to radio propagation. Quite the contrary, however, the external walls help in suppressing interference to the average power level of $-125$ dBm per subcarrier. As regards the transmission mode, the Orthogonal Frequency Division Multiple Access (OFDMA) is employed in the Time Division Duplex (TDD) mode at the carrier frequency of 5.0 GHz with the channel bandwidth of 100 MHz. In particular, each ACN, is assigned a fixed amount of radio resource equal to one chunk being formed of 8 subcarriers and 15 OFDM symbols.

As illustrated in Table 7.1, both the SN and ACNs are equipped with a single omnidirectional antenna each, transmitting with the same power of 21 dBm but differing over the antenna gain, equal to 7 dBi and 0 dBi, respectively. Given the configuration for the network level Cooperation Orchestration Decision Element CO_DE, an AWGN channel characterised by either the A1 Line of Sight (LOS)

**Table 7.1** System parameters

| Parameter | Value | Description |
|---|---|---|
| Carrier frequency | 5.0 GHz | TDD mode |
| Channel bandwidth | 100 MHz | OFDMA |
| Spatial processing | DSTBC | ACN-ACN collaboration |
| SN antennae | 1 | Omnidirectional |
| ACN antennae | 1 | Omnidirectional |
| SN transmit power | 21 dBm | 7 dBi antenna gain |
| ACN transmit power | 21 dBm | 0 dBi antenna gain |
| Channel modelling | AWGN channel | A1 NLOS Room-Room model used for SN-ACN links |
| Link adaptation | Fixed code and modulation scheme | QPSK and (4, 5, 7) convolutional code |
| Mobility | Yes | ACNs |
| Resource scheduling | Fixed | 1 chunk, i.e. 15 OFDM symbols and 8 subcarriers, for each ACN |
| RAP selection | Signal power | At the DN |
| Traffic model | Constant bit rate | CBR |

(6.2) or A1 Non Line-of-Sight (NLOS) (6.3) radio propagation model is applied, depending on the existence of walls across the dynamically formed radio links. Moreover, a fixed modulation and coding scheme is employed based on the QPSK modulation and the (4, 5, 7) convolutional code [14]. The Constant Bit Rate (CBR) traffic model is utilised, while the selection of the ACNs intended to express ACB takes place on the basis of the signal power observed at the Destination Node. The simulations are performed in such a way that a given DN is served cooperatively by two ACNs able to provide the signal of best quality. The switching is performed autonomically as directed by the said CO_DE, introduced in Sect. 6.6. To visualise the performance of such a set-up, first the relative throughput curves and, then, the Cumulative Distribution Functions (CDFs) are juxtaposed for all there layouts to highlight the potential fluctuations arising from the repositioning of the ACNs.

In particular, the relative throughputs for all the layouts A, B, and C, each composed of four configurations, are presented in Fig. 7.5, Fig. 7.6, and Fig. 7.7, respectively [13]. Importantly, the configurations 1, 2, 3, and 4 are arranged in such a way, that the ACNs are located farther from the centre. In fact, none of the arrangements of ACNs may cover the entire area and, thus, autonomic switching is indispensable. Furthermore, the pertinent CDFs indicate, that the layout B and the configurations B.2 and B.3 seem to perform best, overall (Fig. 7.9). While for the layout A of a circular nature, the similarly almost identical configurations A.3 and A.4 are most advantageous (Fig. 7.8), such a deployment appears less

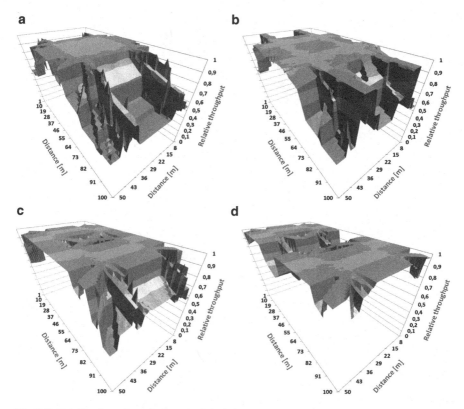

**Fig. 7.5**  Relative throughput for layouts A.1–A.4

efficient compared to the previous one. Finally, the layout C seems also less efficient from this angle, too, and this time the configuration C.3 operates most effectively (Fig. 7.10).

## 7.7   Conclusion

In this chapter, certain dose of relevant insight into the practical side of the proposed concept was provided in the context of implementation and simulation. To this end, first of all the architecture of the developed simulator was introduced to shed additional light on the mutual relations and interactions between the layers of the implemented protocol stack and the levels of abstraction containing the relevant

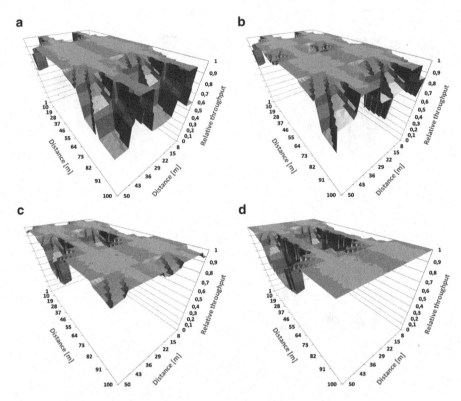

**Fig. 7.6** Relative throughput for layouts B.1–B.4

Decision Elements (DEs). Following, the operational aspects of the functioning
of the protocol itself were presented in the context of explaining their pertinent
encapsulation mechanisms. Based on this, the very concept of multi-threading with
the use of the Java programming language was discussed not only to highlight the
most important assumptions, but, additionally, to show the direct correspondence
between and the notion of Autonomic Cooperative Behaviour (ACB) and the concept of multi-threading. This part was further complemented with the mathematical
analysis of the reception of the signals processed by the Distributed Spatio-Temporal
Block Coding (DSTBC). Finally, the parameters of the assumed scenario were
described together with the corresponding layouts and configurations of ACNs, as
well as the relevant reference simulation results were provided.

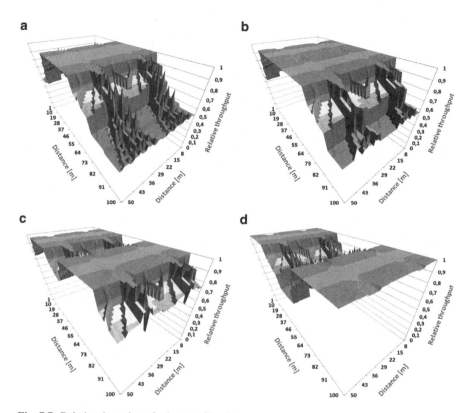

**Fig. 7.7** Relative throughput for layouts C.1–C.4

**Fig. 7.8** CDFs for layouts
A.1–A.4

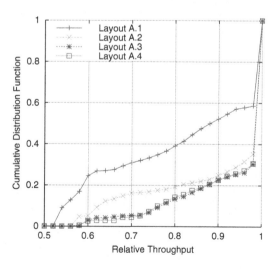

**Fig. 7.9** CDFs for layouts
B.1–B.4

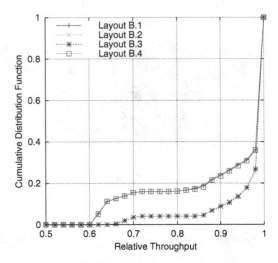

**Fig. 7.10** CDFs for layouts
C.1–C.4

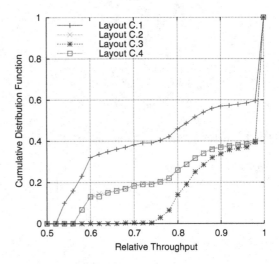

# References

1. Dohler, M., & Li, Y. (2010). *Cooperative communications - hardware, channel & PHY*. UK: John Wiley & Sons.
2. Doppler, K., Redana, S., Wódczak, M., Rost, P., & Wichman, R. (2007). Dynamic resource assignment and cooperative relaying in cellular networks: Concept and performance assessment. *EURASIP Journal on Wireless Communications and Networking, 2009*, 1–14.
3. Eckel, B. (2006). *Thinking in Java* (4th ed.). US: Prentice Hall.
4. Goetz, B., Peierls, T., Bloch, J., Bowbeer, J., Holmes, D., & Lea, D. (2006). *Java concurrency in practice*. US: Addison-Wesley Professional.
5. Jankiraman, M. (2004). *Space-Time codes and MIMO systems*. US: Artech House.
6. Tanenbaum, A. S., & Wetherall, D. J. (2011). *Computer networks*. US: Prentice Hall.
7. Tarokh, V., Jafarkhani, H., & Calderbank, A. R. (1999). Space-time block coding for wireless communications: performance results. *IEEE Journal on Selected Areas in Communications, 17*(3), 451–460.
8. Vucetic, B., & Yuan, J. (2003). *Space-time coding*. UK: John Wiley & Sons.
9. Wódczak, M. (2008). Cooperative relaying in an indoor environment. *ICT Mobile Summit*. Sweden: Stockholm.
10. Wódczak, M. (2011). Aspects of cross-layer design in autonomic cooperative networking. In *IEEE Third International Workshop on Cross Layer Design*. France: Rennes.
11. Wódczak, M. (2011). Autonomic cooperative networking for wireless green sensor systems. *International Journal of Sensor Networks (IJSNet), 10*(1/2), 83–93.
12. Wódczak, M. (2011). Resilience aspects of autonomic cooperative communications in Context of Cloud Networking. In *IEEE First Symposium on Network Cloud Computing and Applications*. France: Toulouse.
13. Wódczak, M. (2012). Autonomic cooperative communications for emergency networks. In *4th IEEE MENS at GLOBECOM 2012*. California: Anaheim.
14. Wódczak, M. (2012). *Autonomic cooperative networking*. New York: Springer.
15. Wódczak, M. (2012). Convergence aspects of autonomic cooperative networks. *International Journal of Information Technology and Web Engineering (IJITWE), 6*(4), 51–62.
16. Wódczak, M. (2012). Simulation environment for autonomic cooperative networking in indoor scenario. In *14th International Conference on Modelling and Simulation (UKSim)*. UK: Cambridge.
17. Wódczak, M., Szott, S., & Chaparadza, R. (2013). Autonomic cooperative behaviour in ETSI AFI scenario for autonomicity enabled Ad-hoc and Mesh network architecture. In *5th IEEE MENS at GLOBECOM 2013*. Atlanta, Georgia.
18. Zheng, Y. R., & Xiao, C. (2003). Simulation models with correct statistical properties for rayleigh fading channels. *IEEE Transactions on Communications, 51*(6), 920–928.

# Chapter 8
# Standardisation and Deployment

## 8.1  Introduction

Following the discussion of the components of the Autonomic Cooperative System Architectural Model (ACSAM) in the prior chapters, especially including the Autonomic Cooperative Networking Protocol (ACNP) along with its pertinent Autonomic Cooperative Behaviour (ACB), as well as complemented with the aspects of implementation and simulation, this chapter is intended to provide the relevant insight into the field of standardisation and deployment. To this end, certain concepts of interest are analysed and the contents is structured in such a way that it opens with more standardisation orientated elements while towards the end it naturally becomes rather shifted towards the issue of deployment. Both the components appear to be sufficiently balanced thanks to the aspect of architectural commonalities. In particular, first of all the question of the Autonomic Future Internet is discussed with a special emphasis being put on the related standardisation within the Industry Specification Group (ISG) on Autonomic network engineering for the self-managing Future Internet (AFI), functioning under the auspices of the European Telecommunications Standards Institute (ETSI). Then, the Machine-to-Machine (M2M) communications are analysed also based on the ETSI standardisation efforts and the concept of Software Defined Networking (SDN) follows, which shifts the focus a little bit towards deployment aspects. After this turning point, both the Emergency Systems and Vehicular Networks are brought up, to outline certain architectural elements as viewed from the deployment angle.

## 8.2  Autonomic Future Internet

The Future Internet is becoming one of the most desirable concepts, sought after by various research and development communities. The interest in this topic, being substantial, seems at least steady if not rapidly increasing, most likely due

M. Wódczak, *Autonomic Computing Enabled Cooperative Networked Design*,
SpringerBriefs in Computer Science, DOI 10.1007/978-1-4939-0764-9_8,
© The Author(s) 2014

to the fact that referring to the future in the very name of the said concept makes it appear continually evolvable and open-ended. This way the drive for innovation is continuous and a wide variety of different incarnations of the Future Internet are being put forward. Essentially, as the foreseen number of devices to be interconnected worldwide is expected to grow more and more drastically, the proposed Autonomic Cooperative System Architectural Model (ACSAM) advocates for a completely autonomic design, allowing for full self-manageability. In fact, as outlined in this book, the notion of self-management is perceived as the key enabler for the instantiation of efficient networking, and the cooperative one in particular. Clearly, given the availability of the enormous addressing space offered by IPv6, it is claimed that the Internet of Things (IoT) will enable virtually any networked element to feature its own Internet Protocol (IP) address. Thus, the density of communication-ready devices will most obviously translate into low power transmission schemes, potentially making the way not only for the Autonomic Cooperative Behaviour (ACB) based Autonomic Cooperative Networking Protocol (ACNP) but the whole ACSAM. To this end, however, a strong standardisation orientated effort in indispensable.

Such an effort has been accordingly undertaken by the Industry Specification Group (ISG) on Autonomic network engineering for the self-managing Future Internet (AFI), operating under the auspices of the European Telecommunications Standards Institute (ETSI) [2].[1] As such, the ETSI ISG AFI was established in response to a commonly agreed consensus that both the prior developments and concepts, as well as the numerous efforts ongoing at that time, intended to achieve the very identical goal of instantiating autonomic and self-managing networking, urgently demanded the relevant dose of harmonisation in the context of the rapidly progressing and advancing design of the Future Internet [18]. Given the above background and reasoning, the structure of the ETSI ISG AFI was arranged according to specific Work Items (WIs) being the basis for the preparation of the ETSI Group Specifications (GSs), to be further upgraded to the ETSI Technical Specifications (TSs). Looking from the present perspective, thus far, the ETSI ISG AFI has finalised the first two ground-laying WIs outlining the scenarios, use cases, and requirements for autonomic/self-managing Future Internet [5], as well as defining an architectural reference model for autonomic networking, cognitive networking, and self-management as required by autonomic network engineering for the self-managing Future Internet [6]. Given the completion of the cited ETSI Work Items, the AFI continues the standardisation process in the area of autonomic reference architectures, analysis of requirements, and specification of implementation-oriented solutions [18].

In particular, the third Work Item was created which is subdivided into the following branches under the titles of "Autonomicity-enabled NGN Reference Architecture (fixed/wired networks)", "Autonomicity-enabled Broadband

---

[1]In fact, since its very co-founding, the author of this book has been actively serving as a Vice-Chairman and Rapporteur of ETSI ISG AFI.

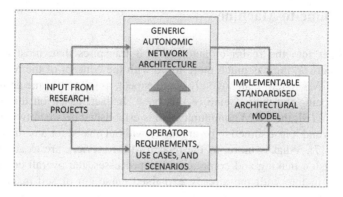

**Fig. 8.1**  AFI standardisation

Forum (BBF) Reference Architecture", "Autonomicity-enabled Mobile Network Architecture (3GPP and Non-3GPP)", as well as "Autonomicity-enabled Wireless Ad-Hoc/Mesh/Sensor Network Architecture".[2,3] Given the fact that the ETSI ISG AFI effort is becoming more and more widespread, certain standardisation methodology was assumed by the body itself [18]. Such a methodology may be perceived a result of the general context of research projects the ETSI ISG AFI was set in from the very outset, as originally it was spawned by the European Union Framework Programme Seven (EU FP7) project on Exposing the Features in IP version Six protocols that can be exploited/extended for the purposes of designing/building Autonomic Networks and Services (EFIPSANS). Consequently, as depicted in Fig. 8.1, the input from the said research projects is welcomed to contribute to the refinement of the Generic Autonomic Network Architecture, as well as the operator requirements, use cases, and scenarios, through a tight interaction between the two relevant WIs. Following, an implementable standardised architectural model is being devised as the main and most comprehensive outcome. In fact, the whole book contains the author's contribution to the instantiation of such a model in the form of ACSAM. The reader is referred to previous chapters for the explanation of the original workings of GANA along with the proposed extensions.

---

[2]The author of this book serves as the Rapporteur of ETSI on the "Autonomicity-enabled Wireless Ad-Hoc/Mesh/Sensor Network Architecture".

[3]As mentioned before, currently, the word "autonomicity" does not seem to exist in the dictionaries of the English language. For this reason, even though this word is now being coined within the ETSI ISG AFI, the author of this book personally avoids using it apart from the officially cited titles of the GSs-to-be. Apart from linguistic purity, however, there indeed appears to exist a semantic gap in this respect and this word might gain common approval much sooner than expected.

## 8.3   Machine-to-Machine

Going further into the realm of automation it transpires that, most obviously,
autonomic networking has much more to do with the concept of the Machine-to-
Machine (M2M) system than anybody could expect, at least from the architectural
perspective being the main theme of this book. In fact, based on the definition
provided by ETSI, the M2M communication is established between two or among
more entities and it is assumed to be organised without a need for any direct human
intervention [7]. What is more, as the related M2M services are to automate the
relevant decision making and communication processes, the overall concept falls
immediately in line with the already explained paradigm of self-manageability,
resembling the operation of the human Autonomic Nervous System (ANS), so
inherent in autonomic networking [18]. Such a characteristic feature is especially
important in the case of highly complex networked systems, where the network
nodes might be represented by M2M devices, and where automation is the only
way forward in terms of a sustainable and durable system operation. The main
components of an M2M system may be decomposed into the ones belonging with
the M2M Device and Gateway, as well as the ones belonging with the M2M
Network [8]. While typically an M2M Device would connect to the network over a
Gateway, a direct connection is also possible, as long as the proper functionality
is properly implemented. The two network related functional blocks deal with
interconnectivity, as opposed to the service layer providing all the abstraction
required for M2M Applications.

   In particular, it is assumed that the primary function of a Machine-to-Machine
Device is to execute the said Machine-to-Machine Applications on the basis of
service capabilities such as certain common functions to be shared after having been
exposed through open interfaces, with the aid of the core network functionality.
Yet, at the same time, it is expected that the workings of the networked parts
of the Machine-to-Machine system be hidden, on its both ends, i.e. the M2M
Device and Gateway, as well as the M2M Network related ones, where the M2M
Applications are residing, as indicated in the latest ETSI Technical Specification
of the Machine-to-Machine functional architecture [8]. Originally, apart from the
collaborative approach to be introduced in the following paragraphs, there are two
aforementioned legacy connection modes. The main difference between the two
consists in the registration, authentication, authorisation, management, and provi-
sioning procedures taking place either directly or with the aid of the Gateway acting
as a Proxy. Interestingly, the networked part pertaining to the M2M Device and
Gateway side is denoted as M2M Area Network which may employ technologies
ranging from Personal Area Networks (PANs) to Local Area Networks (LANs). The
Access Network, in turn, may include both wired and wireless technologies, while
the Core Network is responsible for IP connectivity, roaming, service and network
control functions, as well as interconnection with other networks [8].

As proposed in Fig. 8.2, describing a modified Machine-to-Machine functional architecture, it appears that it would readily accommodate the idea of collaborative transmission which could be taking place mostly between or among the M2M Cooperative Gateways providing the connectivity for the M2M Devices over the M2M Access and Core network. This way, not only would the M2M Gateways become capable of expressing the Autonomic Cooperative Behaviour, but, what is more, the M2M Devices implementing the Gateway functionality could express their willingness to carry and forward traffic. All this remains very much in line with the instantiation of autonomics by means of the Autonomic Cooperative Networking Protocol, as advocated for earlier in this book. Certainly, entering Autonomic Cooperative Behaviour would mean the necessity for the M2M Devices or Gateways to implement the functionality of Autonomic Cooperative Nodes so that the whole set-up could work under the umbrella of the Autonomic Cooperative System Architectural Model. In particular, it looking at the variety of the use cases defined for Machine-to-Machine communications [7], this technology may go hand-in-hand with the Internet of Things, referred to in the previous section, or, at least, become one of its key enablers. This is mostly so because, similarly to the Autonomic Future Internet, the rationale behind Machine-to-Machine is quite generic making both approaches, in some sense, technology agnostic and, thus, highly interoperable, especially when the architectural models are concerned.

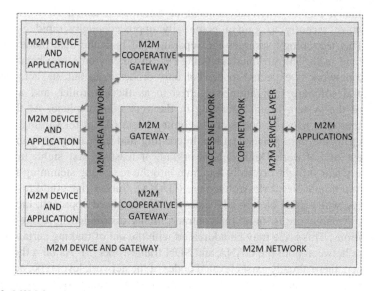

**Fig. 8.2** M2M functional architecture with ACB

## 8.4  Software Defined Networking

Given the already mentioned complexity of the current and future networked systems, quite expectedly, there are other technologies developed entirely with the intention of taking the human out of the configuration and management processes to the highest possible extent, thereby increasing the overall stability and scalability of such advanced designs. Once again, following the rationale behind the Machine-to-Machine and, most importantly, very much as it is the case for autonomics itself, also the concept of Software Defined Networking (SDN) emphasises the fact that the distributed character of today's systems demands certain dose of an urgent intervention in terms facilitating their configurability, not to even mention the related manageability. The reason for such a need may be fairly easily explained on the basis that nowadays the most sophisticated policies and tasks might still be implemented only with the use of the legacy Command Line Interface (CLI), allowing, at most, for the use of a limited set of low-level device configuration directives [9]. Even if it was possible to perform the overall configuration in such a way, the changing state of the continually evolving networked system would still remain not properly addressed. A while ago such a problem seemed to have been solvable with the aid of introducing some automation with the aid of the so-called dynamic scripting approaches but, apparently, taking into account the technological progress, it may no longer be the case.

Most likely, this is why, the concept of Software Defined Networking has emerged most recently to gain a potentially unprecedentedly rapid growth in interest. This technology assumes the separation of both the data plane and the control plane in the current understanding [9]. In other words, the behaviour of the whole network is expected to be, not only orchestrated but, in fact, dictated by a central software programme, referred to as the controller, and assuming the role of the system brain, operating in the very control plane. At the same time, all the other network nodes are becoming basic packet forwarding devices, functioning in the data plane, in turn. Interesting and appealing as it might be, the concept of Software Defined Networking, at least at first sight, might not immediately and straightforwardly integrate into the reasoning stemming from the Generic Autonomic Network Architecture (GANA). Such a risk could result from the fact that while SDN clearly advocates for a centralised approach, the GANA Reference Architecture is, quite the contrary, highly distributed, just like the pre-SDN solutions. This issue may be addressed with the aid of making certain formal alignments between both the GANA and SDN frameworks [3]. As far a the former is concerned, there already exist elevated nodes of the network level type, according to the assumed abstraction, orchestrating their pertinent network domains, while the latter would need to maintain network segmentation with the aid of domain controllers. Given such an assumption, certain simplification to GANA may be proposed, too.

In particular, the programmability offered by SDN comes in handy allowing for run-time software composition. In other words, the elevated Autonomic Cooperative Nodes (ACNs), each assuming the functionality of a controller, may be entitled to execute more complicated programmes in order to fulfil the requirements of the Autonomic Cooperative System Architectural Model (ACSAM), communicated through Autonomic Cooperative Networking Protocol (ACNP). As outlined in Fig. 8.3, in the case of such an SDN-enabled Autonomic Cooperative System Architectural Model, the functionality of plain Autonomic Nodes (ANs) is proposed to be limited up to the function level of the GANA abstraction, while for the Autonomic Cooperative Nodes, intended to express the Autonomic Cooperative Behaviour, the full four-level abstraction would be maintained. In fact, the number of the available levels of abstraction could be part of the said programmability, and once promoted to the role of ACN, the functionality of an AN would become autonomically elevated, which, potentially, would be also the case the other way round. Such a change of role could be triggered by a dynamic network reconfiguration caused, for example, by some external policy-related factors, or be conditioned by an internal shift resulting from the willingness to carry and forward traffic parameter of the Optimised Link State Routing (OLSR) protocol, being the basis for the Autonomic Cooperative Networking Protocol.

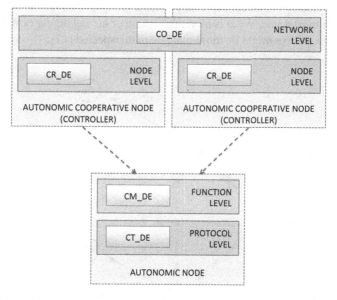

**Fig. 8.3** SDN and ACB

## 8.5  Emergency Systems

Moving a bit from the being standardised architectural components towards a more deployment related context, it appears impossible not to discern the importance of the latest advancement in the development of the novel infrastructure for the emergency system of the future [1]. It is especially conspicuous in the ad hoc or mesh part of such a system, where the devices carried by the First Responders (FRs) seek seamless and on-demand connectivity [12]. For this very reason, emergency networks, formed by such FRs operating in the area of incident, seem to have become a very relevant field for the application of the previously introduced concepts related to the Autonomic Cooperative System Architectural Model (ACSAM). It especially holds true for numerous small groups of FRs, coordinated by their respective Chief First Responders (CFRs), as there appears to arise a correspondence between the topics of human resource and network resource management [11]. Such groups may be assumed to contain from four through six FRs which immediately translates into the following options when the preferred network topology is concerned [14]. In particular, as the FRs would normally gather around the CFR and, most naturally, form the topology of a star, a multi-hop communication between the CFR and its FRs might not be the predominant case. On the other hand, the possibility of instantiating the multi-hop communication cannot be obviously excluded, especially when a group of FRs is more spread apart by forming almost a line. What is more, the option of having bigger or merging and splitting trams of FRs might be more realistic than expected [17].

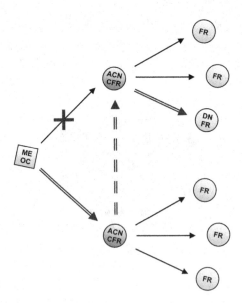

**Fig. 8.4** Supportive cooperation between CFRs acting as ACNs

This brings about the question of how such a system should be orchestrated given the harsh characteristics of the environment it is expected to operate in [15]. In principle, the implementation of the Autonomic Cooperative System Architectural Model, supported by the inclusion of the Autonomic Cooperative Networking Protocol and Autonomic Cooperative Behaviour, seems to be the proper way forward. In fact, one should note that, apart from CFRs and FRs, there also exist both the Emergency Operations Centre (EOC) and the Mobile Emergency Operations Centre (MEOC). While the former is located at a fixed site, the latter is mobile so that it can be relocated to the area of incident. As a result, the cooperation between or among CFRs may be perceived from both the angle of supportive and collaborative protocols, as introduced and defined in Sect. 4.2. Looking from the supportive action perspective, it is typically assumed that the process of communication between two FRs belonging to two separate FR teams would be assisted solely by their respective CFRs, communicating not directly but over the MEOC, as outlined in Fig. 8.4. Such an assumption would need to be relaxed as there may appear a potential lack of communication with the Mobile Emergency Operations Centre, even though such a case would be presumably rare. Moreover, for legacy reasons, related to the hierarchy of a consolidated management of distinct FR teams, it would be required that solely a given CFR can communicate and, thus, route the data coming from the Emergency Operations Centre towards a given FR team.

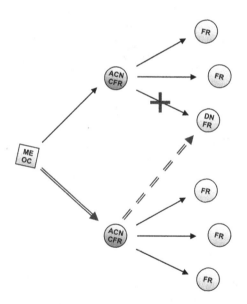

**Fig. 8.5** Back-up operation of supporting CFR

From the Autonomic Cooperative System Architectural Model perspective, however, there are no clear arguments against the establishment of a logical connection over another CFR, as long as such an operation remains transparent to the system, making the human hierarchy look as if nothing had changed. In fact, as outlined in Fig. 8.5, should one of the CFRs be unable to communicate with its FRs, the system would offer support through the autonomic switching to a back-up mode, where another CFR could be exploited as an intermediary entity, allowing for communication with MEOC. In fact, to enable switching between different operation modes, not only would it be necessary to monitor the links between CFRs and their corresponding FRs, but the system would need to be autonomically notified about a potential availability of another CFR to serve the FR or FRs not belonging to his own team [17]. Having the relevant global data related to the network parameters, MEOC would even have some leeway to arrange for collaboration still before link degradation occurs, making the use of the Cooperative Re-Routing Decision Element CR_DE, working closely with the Resilience and Survivability Decision Element RS_DE, as well as the Fault Management Decision Element FM_DE, according to the logic described in Sect. 6.5 [16]. Such an assistance of an external CFR in the communication between MEOC and a given FR, done by means of instantiating the Autonomic Cooperative Behaviour, in a way transparent to the system and not affecting the hierarchy, is presented in Fig. 8.6.

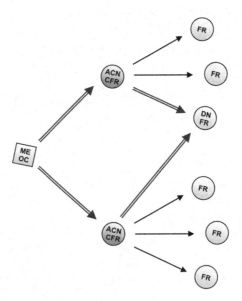

**Fig. 8.6** ACB expressed by two CFRs

## 8.6 Vehicular Networks

As the latest cutting edge technologies for mobile communications, offering better transmission capabilities, are being devised globally, the concept of a world-wide deployment of efficient vehicular systems is becoming more and more crystallised [10]. On the one hand, certain advancement in this direction may be observed both in the case of the Physical Layer, as well as the Medium Access Control Layer, where the emphasis is generally laid on the provision of wider bandwidth and lower transmission latencies. On the other hand, however, one needs to remember about the Network Layer, where the aspects of autonomic networking and collaborative communication seem to gain increasingly significant attention these days. In fact, as advocated for throughout the whole chapter, self-management and autonomics should be perceived as the core elements of the ubiquitous network of the future [4]. Such a ubiquity means, that, undoubtedly, vehicular systems will become the key element of the global networking ecosystem and it is crucial to ensure that the relevant technologies are included in their development from the very outset. A distinctiveness of the vehicular networks may be related to their high complexity in terms of topology control and service provision [10]. Therefore, certain dose of autonomics is required for the purposes of guaranteeing smooth and robust system operation. Primarily, it is expected that there will be a need for the vehicles to express autonomic configuration capabilities in order to address the issues of rapid topology changes and distributed system nature.

**Fig. 8.7** Interaction between DEs and OBU

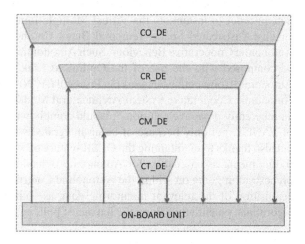

What is more, the very relevant question of self-management needs to be answered so that it would be possible to understand how the networked nodes, i.e. vehicles, can express the Autonomic Cooperative Behaviour and manifest it through, for example, the ability of employing the Autonomic Cooperative Networking Protocol [13]. Undoubtedly, such a system needs to be stable and scalable, and, thus, large-scale vehicular networks should express self-management through efficient and effective self-configuration and self-management so that it would be capable of functioning by itself without any necessity for a specific external human intervention during the majority of its operation time [4]. The incorporation of a relevant communication logic may be facilitated with the aid of the components of the Autonomic Cooperative System Architectural Model (ACSAM) building on top of the notion of the Autonomic Control Loop (ACL) of Generic Autonomic Network Architecture (GANA) [18]. In other words, as outlined in Fig. 8.7, the basic idea would be that the interaction with the GANA Decision Element (DE) is taking place on all the levels, where the ACLs allow to orchestrate their respective Managed Entity (ME), implemented within the On-Board Unit (OBU). A question may arise, however, in what way should the On-Board Unit be perceived when it comes to the interfacing with the Autonomic Cooperative System Architectural Model, as, in general, it would seem that it could be treated as a Managed Entity on some level of the Generic Autonomic Network Architecture abstraction.

In fact, as such, the On-Board Unit appears to be much more of a networked device, featuring certain dose of additional capabilities. This way, being rather a composition of various protocols and manageable routines, the On-Board Unit should not be seen as a singe Managed Entity. Quite the contrary, similarly to network routers, the Autonomic Cooperative System Architectural Model would need to be then integrated into the OBU in order to orchestrate its operation from the inside. This way, going through various levels of abstraction, the vehicles of a Vehicular Ad-hoc NETwork (VANET) would be able to form Virtual Cooperative Sets in order to instantiate the Virtual Multiple Input Multiple Output technology enabled Distributed Spatio-Temporal Block Coding for the needs of expressing Autonomic Cooperative Behaviour. Such Autonomic Cooperative Behaviour would be composed with the use of the Optimised Link State Routing (OLSR) based Autonomic Cooperative Networking Protocol (ACNP) under the overall umbrella of Autonomic Cooperative System Architectural Model. Particularly, as the ACNP is an inherently proactive solution, it would comply with the autonomic environment of VANET, not only because of being integrated with collaborative transmission, but also thanks to maintaining the OLSR feature of willingness to carry and forward traffic, meant as an enabler for Autonomic Behaviour (AB), in general [10]. The orchestration going on within the Autonomic Control Loop would then involve the acquisition of the relevant monitoring data, as well as the application of certain algorithms, potentially having the flavour of policies [17].

## 8.7  Conclusion

In this chapter, the relevant insight into the field of standardisation and deploy-ment was provided. For this reason, the concepts of interest analysed in the consecutive sections were structured accordingly, so that the whole chapter could have been opened with the rather standardisation orientated topics, while towards the end it started naturally becoming to lean towards the issue of deployment. An utmost attention was paid to present both the components in a sufficiently balanced manner. Such a presentation was facilitated by the fact of the existence of numerous architectural commonalities. In particular, first the phenomenon of the Autonomic Future Internet was discussed with a special emphasis having been laid on the related standardisation within the ISG AFI, operating under the auspices of the European Telecommunications Standards Institute. Then, the Machine-to-Machine (M2M) communications were analysed mostly on the basis of the ETSI standardisation efforts and the concept of Software Defined Networking (SDN) followed, which shifted the focus more towards the deployment aspects. Eventually, both the Emergency Systems and Vehicular Networks were brought up, to outline certain architectural advancements as viewed from the deployment perspective.

# References

1. Calarco, G., Casoni, M., Paganelli, A., Vassiliadis, D., & Wódczak, M. (2010). A satellite based system for managing crisis scenarios: the E-SPONDER perspective. In *5th Advanced Satellite Multimedia Systems Conference*. Italy: Cagliari.
2. Chaparadza, R., Ciavaglia, L., Wódczak, M., Chen, C.-C., Lee, B. A., Liakopoulos, A., et al. (2009). ETSI industry specification group on autonomic network engineering for self-managing future internet (ETSI ISG AFI). In G. Vossen, D. Long, & J. Yu (Eds.), *Springer Lecture Notes in Computer Science (LNCS): Web Information Systems Engineering* (Vol. 5802/2009). *10th International Conference on Web Information Systems Engineering* Poland: Poznań.
3. Chaparadza, R., Meriem, T. B., Radier, B., Szott, S., Wódczak, M, Prakash, A., et al. (2013). SDN enablers in the ETSI AFI GANA reference model for autonomic management and control (emerging standard), and virtualization impact. In *5th IEEE MENS at GLOBECOM 2013*. Atlanta: Georgia.
4. Chaparadza, R., Papavassiliou, S., Kastrinogiannis, T., Vigoureux, M., Dotaro, E., Davy, A., et al. (2009). Creating a viable evolution path towards self-managing future internet via a standardizable reference model for autonomic network engineering. In G. Tselentis, J. Domingue, A. Galis, A. Gavras, D. Hausheer, S. Krco, V. Lotz, and T. Zahariadis (Eds.) *Chapter in the book: "Towards the Future Internet - A European Research Perspective"* IOS Press, ISBN: 978-1-60750-007-0. Also published at the Future Internet Assembly 2009 in Prague.
5. ETSI GS AFI 001 V1.1.1. (2011). *Autonomic network engineering for the self-managing Future Internet (AFI); scenarios, use cases and requirements for autonomic/self-managing future internet*. ETSI Group Specification, France.
6. ETSI GS AFI 002 V1.1.1. (2013). *Autonomic network engineering for the self-managing future internet (AFI); generic autonomic network architecture (an architectural reference model for autonomic networking, cognitive networking and self-management)*. ETSI Group Specification, France.
7. ETSI TS 102 689 V1.1.1. (2010). *Machine-to-machine communications (M2M); M2M service requirements*. ETSI Technical Specification, France.
8. ETSI TS 102 690 V2.1.1. (2013). *Machine-to-machine communications (M2M); functional architecture*. ETSI Technical Specification, France.

9. Hyojoon K., & Feamster, N. (2013). Improving network management with software defined networking. *IEEE Communications Magazine, 51*(2), 114–119.

10. Li, J., Wódczak, M., Wu, X., & Hsing, T. R. (2012). Vehicular networks and applications – challenges, requirements and service opportunities. *Academy Publisher Journal of Communications (JCM), 7*(5), 365–373.

11. Vassiliadis, D., Garbi, A., Calarco, G., Casoni, M., Paganelli, A., Morera, R., et al. (2010). Wireless networks at the service of effective first response work: the E-SPONDER vision. In *EEE International Symposium on Wireless Pervasive Computing*. Italy: Modena.

12. Wódczak, M. (2011). Autonomic cooperation in Ad-hoc environments. In *5th International Workshop on Localised Algorithms and Protocols for Wireless Sensor Networks (LOCALGOS) in conjunction with IEEE International Conference on Distributed Computing in Sensor Systems (DCOSS)*. Spain: Barcelona.

13. Wódczak, M. (2011). Autonomic cooperative networking for wireless green sensor systems. *International Journal of Sensor Networks (IJSNet), 10*(1/2), 83–93.

14. Wódczak, M. (2011). Deployment aspects of autonomic cooperative communications in emergency networks. In *3rd International Congress on Ultra Modern Telecommunications and Control Systems, IEEE ICUMT*. Hungary: Budapest.

15. Wódczak, M. (2011). Resilience aspects of autonomic cooperative communications in context of cloud networking. In *IEEE First Symposium on Network Cloud Computing and Applications*. France: Toulouse.

16. Wódczak, M. (2012). Autonomic cooperative communications for emergency networks. In *4th IEEE MENS at GLOBECOM 2012*. Anaheim: California.

17. Wódczak, M. (2012). *Autonomic cooperative networking*. New York: Springer.

18. Wódczak, M., Meriem, T. B., Radier, B., Chaparadza, R., Quinn, K., Kielthy, J., et al. (2011). Standardizing a reference model and autonomic network architectures for the self-managing future internet. *IEEE Network, 25*(6), 50–56.

# Chapter 9
# Summary

In this book a comprehensive architectural design of a complex and convergent autonomic cooperative networked system was proposed, intended to weld the realms of computing and networking closely together. In fact, being a multi-faceted solution, the outlined design highly capitalised on the groundbreaking concept of autonomic computing, as such being based on the idea of the transposition of the human Autonomic Nervous System into the architecture able to efficiently manage the operation of complex computer systems. Not only were the key aspects of autonomic computing itself explained, but most importantly, the conceptual changes were indicated to settle the ground for the introduction of the new concept of Autonomic Cooperative System Architectural Model. In particular, special emphasis was laid on exposing the novelty of the ACSAM in relation to the Generic Autonomic Network Architecture, with an utmost attention having been paid to the bottom-up analysis of Autonomic Control Loops (ACLs) operating on various levels of abstraction. As a result, the key components of the said ACSAM, in the form of the Autonomic Cooperative Networking Protocol and Autonomic Cooperative Behaviour, were introduced and the reader was familiarised with the key concept of Autonomic Cooperative Node as the main enabler for the instantiation of the said ACB. Following, the details of the very concept of ACB, constituting the lowest level of the three-tier ACSAM and designed to be composed with the aid of creating Virtual Cooperative Sets being orchestrated by the Autonomic Cooperative Networking Protocol, were given. In fact, not only was the ACB found many-faceted but, especially, also hardly definable. To account for its role and meaning, the notion of collaborative and supportive protocols was introduced, the Virtual Multiple Input Multiple Output channel was defined as its enabler through Distributed Spatio-Temporal Block Coding over VCSs and with the aid of the Multi-Point Relay station selection heuristics of the Optimised Link State Routing protocol. Based on this, the workings of the Autonomic Cooperative Networking Protocol were outlined as being a cross-layer solution combining certain aspects of both the Network and Link Layers, while, in fact, going even down to the Physical Layer for the needs of orchestrating the underlying VMIMO. In particular, the relevant

M. Wódczak, *Autonomic Computing Enabled Cooperative Networked Design*,
SpringerBriefs in Computer Science, DOI 10.1007/978-1-4939-0764-9_9,
© The Author(s) 2014

context of the reference OLSR protocol was presented and the integration of ACB was described keeping in mind the role of MPR station selection heuristics. This part was complemented with the proposed messaging structure and the functioning of ACNP itself in terms of assigning ACNs to VCSs. Eventually, the analysis of the expected overhead induced by the OLSR-ACNP tandem was provided, too. Given the above context, the relevant Decision Making Entities were introduced to complement the overall design of ACSAM. First, the Cooperative Transmission Decision Element CT_DE was deployed at the protocol level to orchestrate the VMIMO enabled DSTBC. Following, certain logic was elevated to the function level, where the Cooperation Management Decision Element CM_DE was positioned being responsible for the interaction with the ACNP for the needs of enabling the MPR-based DSTBC. Moving up to the node level, the Cooperative Re-Routing Decision Element CR_DE was introduced as being responsible for triggering the cooperative re-routing procedure to guarantee service continuity, and, last but not least, the Cooperation Orchestration Decision Element CO_DE was defined to be responsible for arranging various ACB accordingly. As a next step, the implementation and simulation related aspects of the ACSAM were analysed. To this end, the architecture of the developed simulator was introduced along with the operational aspects of the protocol itself. Based on this, the concept of multi-threading with the use of the Java programming language was discussed to show its direct correspondence with ACB. This part was further complemented with the mathematical analysis of the reception of the DSTBC, and, finally, the parameters of the assumed scenario were described together with the corresponding layouts of ACNs and the reference simulation results. Eventually, both the standardisation and deployment orientated approaches were scrutinised. First, the Autonomic Future Internet was discussed with the emphasis put on standardisation within the Industry Specification Group (ISG) on Autonomic network engineering for the self-managing Future Internet (AFI) functioning under the auspices of the European Telecommunications Standards Institute (ETSI). Then, the Machine-to-Machine (M2M) communications were analysed in the very same context of ETSI and the concept of Software Defined Networking (SDN) followed. Last but not least, both the Emergency Systems and Vehicular Networks were brought up to present their pertinent architectural advancements from the deployment viewpoint.